THE LAST TIME

ERICK WILLIAMS

CHAPTER ONE

Sixteen-year-old Nick Graham drives his gray 2006 Honda Accord, up to the drive-thru menu at Burger House. He is a coca brown brother with a Mohawk fade haircut and wears a diamond stud in his left ear. A teenage female comes over the loudspeaker says, "We will be with you in a minute."

Spenser Green his partner is also 5'11" he is seventeen years old, slightly darker, with a low drop fade and short afro twist. He has on a pair of Nike black full-rim rectangular glasses. He leans over from the passenger side and yells, "Yo is Jordan here?"

The same girl comes over the speaker, "What?" Nick pushes Spenser back to the passenger seat, asks, "Jordan Skyy is he working?"

The girl answers back over the speaker, "Jordan yeah, he's out in the lobby cleaning up, we're about to close in 15 minutes."

Nick responds, "Hold on we coming around."

Nick drives around to the window, the girl is another teenager with long brunette hair past her shoulder it's tied in a ponytail, she is wearing sterling silver hoop earrings. Spenser leans over towards Nick tells her, "Damn you fine. Can I hit you up on Instagram?"

"I don't think so," she answers and she shuts the window.

Nick and Spenser both yell, "Hold up, hold up," she comes back and opens the window replies, "Look I don't have time to play, we about to close."

Nick laughs, "Aight aight can you go get Jordan for us?"

She shuts the window and walks away. Spenser asks, "You think she went to get him?" Nick, "I don't know, I guess we can wait a few minutes."

Spenser rubs his hands together, "Man I'm hungry I hope he can hook us up."

After about a five-minute wait, Spenser tells Nick, "Let's go man we still trying to get to this party."

Nick puts the car in drive and is about to take off when the drive-through window opens up and Jordan Skyy he is also a sixteen-year-old, 6'0"papersack brown brother with braids on the top and faded on the side yells, "What you fools doing here?"

Nick answers, "Yo we going to Chloe's party you down?"

Jordan replies, "Of course bro let me clock out, I'll be out in two minutes."

Spenser, "Aight fool hurry up." Jordan shuts the window. Nick starts the car and pulls up to the door. Jordan runs out and jumps in the back seat. Nick drives away.

Spenser in the front seat, reaches back shakes his hand, "What up J? You ready to get lit?"

Jordan excitedly answers, "Yeah, but I need to text my mom to let her know she doesn't need to pick me up."

Spenser comments, "Bro you smell like burgers, you couldn't hook us up?"

"If you had come 30 minutes earlier maybe. Chill for a minute so I can text my mom."

Jordan text: *You don't need to pick me up, I got a ride from Nick.*

Spenser takes a joint from his shirt pocket and he lights it up, takes a long hit says, "Welcome to the zoot box" as he blows the smoke out, Jordan taps him on the shoulder tells him, "Yo pass it back."

Spenser, "Aight dog, chill" as he is still blowing out the smoke. He knocks the ash from it into an empty water bottle.

Jordan's phone plays, "Dear mama" the 2Pac song, he pulls it out of his pocket it's his mom Vicky, Jordan yells, "Chill fools it's my mom."

Vicky says, *"I wish you would have called me earlier, I'm already on my way."*

Jordan replies, *"My bad they just showed up."*

"Who are they?"

"I'm with Nick and Spenser, we headed to a party."

"So, are you asking or telling me?"

Jordan responds with, *"I thought you already said it was cool."*

"I don't remember talking about it."

Jordan *"It's Chloe's party, I won't be out too late."*

Vicky sighs, *"Alright don't get into any trouble."*

Jordan hangs up the phone, "Aight now pass the blunt."

Spenser passes it back to Jordan, he takes a hit and starts coughing, both Nick and Spenser laugh, Nick, "Damn dude, slow down and breathe."

Jordan still coughing answers, "I'm good." He passes it to Nick, "Yo so where is this party at?"

Spenser answers, "Hills Point Projects."

Nick takes a hit off the joint and passes it back to Spenser.

Spenser hits the joint and passes it back to Jordan, Jordan hits it again, holds the joint out in front looks at it trying to hold the smoke in gagging says, "This is some good shit."

Spenser and Nick start laughing. Nick, "Don't you know rule number one, don't start a conversation holding the blunt, now pass it" he playfully snatches it from Jordan.

Jordan still gagging passes the joint to Nick, takes the hit, passes it to Spenser he takes one long toke and holds the smoke in, gags lets it out, and puts the joint butt into the water bottle.

Nick turns left into the Hills Point projects and asks, "What apartment?"

Jordan answers, "I don't know just listen for the music and look for cars."

"How you feel?" Spenser asks looking back at Jordan.

Jordan laughs his eyes are droopy and bloodshot, chuckles, "I'm feeling good bro."

Nick, "There's Romeo," he points at a guy getting out of a car in the next building over, "That must be where the party is at."

Nick drives up and parks behind Romeo's car. Romeo gets out of the car; he is by himself. Nick, Spenser, and Jordan get out.

They all walk over, Romeo asks, "What's up?"

Spenser replies, "What up? This where Chloe's party at?"

Romeo answers, "Yeah, I just got here too," he sniffs the air, "I see y'all been firing it up."

Spenser shrugs, "Whatever bro, it's a party, let's get lit.

"Where is Jordan?" asks KJ. He is Jordan's 13-year-old younger brother. He is 5'4" with the same complexion as Jordan and they even share the same hairstyle with braids on the top and faded on the side. He is a little short for his age and has the little man syndrome about it.

"He went to a party with his friends," Vicky their mom answers she is 5'7", slightly darker cocoa powder brown, her black hair is styled in tousled curls barely touching her shoulders. She is a thirty-eight-year-old single mom of three, a former high school track and basketball athlete, but life and having kids, has given her the middle age mom body and she is cool with it.

"He promised me that we would play Madden when he got off work."

Vicky, "I'm sorry," she sees the disappointment, in his face asks, "You want me to play?"

"Really mom? You don't even know how to play."

Vicky laughs, "I was just asking."

"I will just play the computer."

"Alright, whatever makes you happy" she sits down on the couch and turns on the TV.

A car turns into the driveway. Vicky thinks *I wonder who this is?*

There is a knock on the door, "Who is it?" she yells from the couch.

"It's Keith open up," says a man's voice from outside.

Vicky asks, "Why are you here?"

Keith pleads, "Come on baby open the door, I just want to talk."

Vicky gets up and opens the door, "So why are you here? You need to call before you just drop by."

Keith is Jordan and KJ's father. He is thirty-seven years old, an assistant manager at a car dealership. He is a 6'0" brother with cornrow braids and a beard he weighs 180lbs. He works out 2 to 3 times a week to maintain his weight, he is all about trying to maintain his looks to impress the ladies. "I just was in the neighborhood and wanted to stop by. Is that cool?"

Vicky smells alcohol as he passes by her and walks into the house, she inquires, "You been drinking?"

KJ hears Keith's voice and comes out of his room, "What's up dad?"

Keith and KJ dap each other up, "What's up junior? How's it going?"

KJ answers, "I'm cool just in my room playing madden. Why are you here?"

Keith a little irritated by the question responds, "Can't a man come by to check on his family?"

Vicky replies, "Now you want to act like we are a family? Where was the family man when we were together? KJ say goodnight to your father."

KJ pleading, "Can he stay, and play madden with me?"

"I think it's best if he leaves."

Keith looks at Vicky, "Just give me a chance."

Vicky tells KJ, "Go to your room, I need to talk to him alone."

KJ puts his head down and slowly walks to his room. Keith sees his disappointment and tells him. "I will see you later junior."

Vicky asks, "What do you want?"

"Like I said I was in the neighborhood and stopped by." He walks towards her with his arms extended to hug her, she puts her right hand out touching his chest stopping him from getting any closer.

"You for real? You come over here drunk, trying to get some? Those days are done."

"They don't have to be if you give me a chance."

"What part of this don't you understand?" She moves her hand back and forth between herself and Keith "This is over, I don't want my kids to get any ideas."

"You mean our kids?"

"You can't just be dropping by at any time wanting to play daddy whenever it is convenient for you. Goodnight Keith."

She walks and opens the front door. Keith walks to the door slowly shaking his head up and down, "Aight it's like that, but remember this not working is not all on me."

CHAPTER TWO

Spenser, Jordan, Nick walk into the apartment, the party is packed, people are everywhere there is a speaker with the lights strobing in rhythm with the music, they walk into the apartment Spenser pokes Jordan with his elbow and says, "Yo this shit is turnt up. I'm getting a beer," he walks to the kitchen.

Nick sees a girl from school he knows, walks towards her, "Later bros."

Jordan sees Chloe she is 5'7" dark-skinned with shoulder-length black hair layered up with red streaks. She's wearing a black baseball cap backward with 2 cherry hearts emblems, and a pair of red dangling rose earrings. Chloe sees Jordan coming and yells to him over the music, "What's up Jordan glad you could make it to my party."

Jordan yells back, "So what's the reason for the party. Is it your birthday?"

Chloe shakes her head no and yells, "No, summer break."

Spenser comes up behind Jordan and gives him a beer, "Yo man have a beer."

Jordan takes the beer and starts to chug it. Spenser chugs his beer and tells Chloe "Lit party girl I didn't know you like to party."

Chloe leans in toward him and whispers, "That's because you never talk to me at school."

Spenser looks at her, "Well I'm here now so what's up?"

A tall slim light-skinned girl approaches Chloe from the other side, she immediately catches Jordan's eye. She is 5'10" with mahogany hair in a high ponytail tied together with a red bow. She is wearing a red dress that stops just above her knees with a small backpack shoulder bag and a pair of red and black air Jordan OG's. She asks Chloe "What's up?" Chloe laughs, "What's up Purple Reign?"

Jordan checking her out asks Chloe, "Purple Reign? What's up with that?"

Chloe answers, "Her name is Reign, You know the old Prince movie, she goes to Bryant their colors are purple and yellow, get it?"

Jordan has a small laugh, "Oh I get it."

Spenser, "So how do y'all know each other?"

"We play summer ball together."

"You play summer ball?" Spenser asks surprised, as he turns up his beer.

"Been playing for 2 years" Chloe answers.

Drinking the rest of his beer he tells Jordan, "J finish it I'll get you another."

"Let's go," he tells Chloe.

Chloe to Reign, "You cool?"

Reign looks at Jordan smiles at him and replies to Chloe, "I'm good."

Spenser and Chloe walk away. Jordan sipping on the beer, asks Reign, "So you play ball at Bryant?"

Reign, "Yeah, I'm the starting shooting guard."

Jordan, "Ok that's cool, yeah I ball a little we gonna have to get on the court to see what you got."

Reign shakes her head in agreement, "No problem."

Spenser comes back with another beer, "Here bro drink up."

Jordan opens it up and takes a gulp. Chloe asks Reign, "So you playing again this summer?"

Reign, "I should be able to I might miss a few games. We moving sometime this summer."

Chloe, "We should have a good squad if everybody comes back."

Spenser interrupts, "Ok, ok enough about balling," looks at Chloe "I was hoping to get to know you better, let's let them talk." He puts his arm around Chloe and they walk away.

Jordan looks at Reign and asks, "So y'all moving this summer, out of town?"

Reign, "No, we not moving out of town we just need a bigger house."

"Ok cool, cool, so what grade you in?"

"I'm a junior, what about you?"

"Same." He takes a big gulp of beer.

Reign watches him and advises, "You might want to be careful."

"No worries, I'm good."

Jordan, "So you seeing anybody?"

Reign, "Yeah"

Jordan surprised by this, "Is he here?"

Reign "No, he is at home he doesn't know I'm here."

Jordan, "Well it can't be that strong if you are here talking to me."

Reign smiles and answers, "Ain't no harm in having a conversation, right? So, you seeing anyone?"

"We broke up it just wasn't meant to be," he answers as he is finishing off his beer.

Jordan, "I'm getting another beer do you want something to drink?"

Reign, "No I'm driving, you really putting them away. Do you always drink like this?"

Jordan doesn't answer her directly he gives her a sly look and responds, "So you're a good girl, huh, I'll be right back."

Jordan walks into the kitchen, and a dude he does not know pulls a chair from the table, stands on it, and says, loudly, "Alright we bout to play Edward Beercans. The rules are simple you have a tall boy taped to each hand and the person who finishes drinking both cans first wins."

Spenser and Nick, come up behind him as the rules are being explained, Spenser "Y'all down to do it?"

Nick, "Naw dog, I'm driving."

Spenser looks at Jordan, "I know you down."

Jordan thinks for a few seconds, "Aight I'm in."

Spenser steps in between Jordan and Nick, and yells, "Me and my boy Jordan are in."

The dude jumps off the chair, "Come on let's go!"

Spenser taps Jordan on the shoulder, "You ready let's do it."

Spenser walks over with Jordan right behind him, two other dudes follow behind them. The dude pulls two six-packs of 16 oz. beers from a cooler. One of the dudes from behind Jordan asks, "Yo ain't we supposed to be doing this with 40s?"

"You got eight bottles of 40 money?" the boy in the chair asks.

Spenser "Let's go." He pulls two cans off the six-pack, "Tape me up."

The dude grabs some gray masking tape and tapes the beer to his hands. Jordan grabs two beers and his hands are taped. The dude tapes the last 2 guys, he then goes by and pulls the tab on everybody's can and yells, "GO!"

CHAPTER THREE

The four of them start chugging their cans, the dude who asked the question pulls back first. Spenser sees this so he stops drinking. Jordan stops chugging and sits in the chair. Jordan looks at Spenser asks him, "Bet you $10 I finish before you do."

Spenser, "Let's go" he then turns up his can taped to his right hand.

Jordan turns up the can on his left hand and he finishes it before Spenser. Jordan slams the empty can on the table and yells, "Halfway home."

Spenser drinks his right-hand can and finishes it, he slams it on the table proclaims, "It ain't over yet."

Jordan stands back up, "Yeah it is" he starts drinking the can on his right hand.

Spenser starts on his second can. Jordan pulls up and takes a seat, he suddenly starts to vomit and he puts his hand over his mouth but the beer can taped to it and stops him from covering it, he tries to hold it in, the beer spills out of his mouth. Everybody in the kitchen yells at him. Chloe hears this and runs to the kitchen, yells, "Damn! Not on the floor, y'all done. Game over."

Spenser yells to Jordan, "You owe me 10."

Jordan's head is down on the edge of the table he's looking at the floor breathing heavily asks, "How you figure? You didn't finish either."

"No problem." He turns up the beer can and finishes the last of it, "Now it's done."

Jordan raises his head, off the table "Get these damn cans off my hand."

The dude comes over with some scissors and cuts the tape, Jordan yells, "Yo Nick we need to go I ain't feeling too good."

Nick walks over to Jordan, Jordan attempts to stand up and his legs buckle Nick catches him. Nick tells him, "Yo dog take it easy."

Nick tells Spenser, "Help me take him to the car."

Spenser approaches from the left side and grabs Jordan, "Yo hold up let me holla at Reign real quick."

Nick replies, "She left about 10 minutes ago. I saw her on the phone and she seemed pretty upset when she left."

Jordan frustrated, "Damn I didn't get her number."

Nick, "Don't sweat it, she and Chloe cool, maybe she can hook you up." Jordan's head is down, as he is being carried out by Nick and Spenser. He mumbles, "Let's go man."

In the car, Jordan's laying down in the back seat, "Yo I can't go home like this, my mom will kill me. Can I stay with one y'all tonight?"

Nick driving answers, "You can chill with me for tonight. I will drop you off early before anybody wakes up at your house."

The next morning Jordan slowly opens the front door, Vicky is asleep on the couch, she hears the front door open, and springs up, sees Jordan, and exclaims, "What the hell do you think you're doing staying out all night."

Jordan surprised, "Oh I didn't know you were up."

Vicky sits up, "You ain't grown you can't be coming in anytime you want."

Jordan answers, "I was trying to leave but Nick, was drinking and we didn't want to chance it with him driving drunk."

Vicky angrily responds, "You must think you're grown, going to a party where there is alcohol and then staying out all night. So how did you get home?"

"Nick woke up early and gave me a ride. I don't know why you are making such a big deal about it."

"I'm making such a big deal because you are a 16-year-old boy, who thinks he's grown and got all the answers."

Jordan mutters, "Maybe I do," as he walks to his room.

Vicky gets up off the couch, asks loudly, "What was that you said?"

Jordan louder answers, "I said maybe I do."

"Don't talk back to me, if you got all the answers, why are you still here? Get out while you still know everything."

"I will."

"So, what are you waiting for?"

KJ hears, the arguing and comes out of his room asks, "Why is everybody yelling?"

Vicky in a calmer voice, "It's ok, me and Jordan were just talking, I'm sorry if we woke you up."

KJ asks Jordan, "So what happened we were supposed to play Madden last night?"

Jordan, "I forgot, I got invited to a party last night, I promise we will play today."

KJ looks at him and tells him, "Aight you promise."

Jordan goes to his room, "I'm going to sleep we will play when I wake up."

Vicky asks KJ, "So what do you want for breakfast?"

KJ's shaking Jordan's bed, "Jordan, Jordan, you sleep?"

Jordan, groggily turns over, "What? What time is it?"

KJ, "It's 2:30, you said we were gonna play Madden today."

Jordan sits up in the bed asks, "Where's mom?"

KJ, "She went shopping. You gonna play or what?"

Jordan, "Chill bro, just give me a second, let me wake up."

KJ walks out of the room excitedly says, "Aight I'm a turn the game on."

Jordan stands up and stretches his arms over his head, "I'll be there in a few minutes." He walks to his dresser looking for his phone it is not there, he looks for it on his bed, he cannot find it, he yells, "KJ call my phone."

He hears the phone ringing, it is coming from the pants he had on last night they are on the floor right beside the bed. "I got it, thanks."

KJ yells back, "Hurry up."

Jordan pulls the phone out of his left front pocket. He checks it and sees Nick has texted him 45 minutes earlier, *what's up you got plans?*

Jordan texting back: *My fault, I'm just waking up. Not feeling too good, dealing with a hangover, just at the house bout to play Madden with KJ. What's up?"*

He walks to KJ's room, "Aight let's go." KJ responds, "Holdup it's still loading."

KJ, "So how was the party last night?"

Jordan, "I drank too much, and got sick and puked."

KJ, "So is that why you didn't come home last night?"

Jordan, "Yeah and I knew it was past my curfew and mom would jump my ass if I came home drunk." KJ laugh.

Jordan, "So you think that's funny?" he playfully pushes him off the bed. "Why is it taking so long for this game to load up?"

KJ presses buttons on the controller and replies, "I don't know what the problem is."

Jordan's phone buzzes, the text reads: *On the way.*

Jordan text back: *Aight, bout to put on some clothes.*

Jordan puts the controller down, "Man we need to get you another game."

"Yeah I know, I told mom and she says we don't have the money."

"Do you know when she is coming back?"

"I don't know, she said probably no longer than an hour. Why?"

Jordan answers, "Nick and Spenser are on their way over, we about to hang, text her to see if she is on her way back."

Jordan gets up and walks to his room and starts to get dressed. KJ yells to Jordan, "She texted that she is putting the bags in the car and that she should be here in 15 minutes."

Nick's text: *I'm outside let's go.*

Jordan texts back: *Aight give me a second.*

Jordan walks to KJ's room asks, "Yo momma on the way back, right?"

KJ is playing the PS 4, "I got the game loaded, let's play."

Jordan, "I'm out Nick and Spenser are waiting."

KJ in a whiney voice complains, "You said you were gonna play, you lied again."

Jordan says, "I promise we will play when I get back."

KJ mumbles, "Yeah right, what am I supposed to tell her when she asks where you at?"

Jordan walks to the living room, "Tell her the truth, you don't know, Peace."

CHAPTER FOUR

Vicky pulls into the driveway, gets out of the car grabs a few bags from the front seat she struggles to the door she opens it yells, "KJ, Jordan come help me with the bags."

KJ puts the controller down comes out of the room answers, "Jordan ain't here."

Vicky drops the bags at the front door and yells, "What!! He left you here by yourself. Where did he go?"

KJ shrugs, "I don't know he left about 15 minutes ago."

Vicky picks the bags up and walks to the kitchen, sighs, "Alright let's get the bags in I will deal with him later."

Nick is driving Spenser's in the passenger seat, Jordan's in the back he asks, "So where we headed?"

Spenser, "Yo can we go by Chloe's place. I feel bad about messing it up last night."

Jordan surprised by this, "Really when did you become so caring?"

Nick sarcastically, "Please he is just trying to get with her."

Spenser laughs, "Is there anything wrong with that? Let's go besides maybe Reign is over."

Jordan is excited by this, "Let's go."

"Is she even home? "Nick asks.

Spenser, "I don't know I didn't get her number, let's just roll through."

Nick drives to Chloe's apartment. All three get out, Spenser knocks on the door.

Chloe answers the door surprised to see them she asked, "Oh what's up?"

Spenser, "We just came by to help you clean up."

Jordan, "Especially since I got sick last night and threw up everywhere."

Chloe opens the door wider, "Sure I can use the help."

They walk into the apartment and it looks like a dump, there are a bunch of red solo cups and about 30 empty beer cans on the living room floor and coffee table. There are Potato chips and popcorn all over the floor. They all walk into the living room and look around Nick shakes his head and says, "Damn this place is trashed."

Chloe sarcastically, "Thanks I hadn't noticed I need to get this place straighten up my parents are coming home tonight."

Spenser asks Chloe, "So what do you want us to do?"

Chloe thinking replies, "Let's split up me and Spenser will clean the kitchen you two start in the living room."

Nick and Jordan look at each other and chuckle, Spenser and Chloe walk to the kitchen, Jordan asks, "Can we get a trash can for the living room?"

Chloe from the kitchen answers, "Sure come get it."

Jordan walks to the kitchen and Chloe grabs a big black 30 gallon can, she gives it to him he asks, "So what's up with your girl Reign?"

Chloe looks at him, "She is cool, she has a boyfriend Dejuan or DJ, he's a jealous asshole, and I don't like him."

Jordan inquires, "So how is their ship?"

Chloe replies, "It's been on and off, I don't know what's going on with them."

Jordan asks, "So when you going to see her again?"

Chloe, "We are supposed to start summer ball practice in a few weeks probably then if she plays."

Jordan takes the trash can to the living room, "Let her know I asked about her."

Spenser yells from the kitchen, "Come on bro start cleaning. You wasting time."

"Dear Mama" starts playing on Jordan's phone he pulls it out, looks at the screen he continues to stare at it while it is playing, he takes a deep breath and answers it.

Vicky at home sitting at the kitchen table, *"Where you at? I can't believe you left your brother here by himself."*

Jordan walks outside the apartment answers her, *"He said he texted you and that you were on your way home."*

"That doesn't make a difference, you should not have left your brother by himself, I could have had an accident or something, or somebody might have broken in the house. Where are you at? You need to come home now."

Jordan *"I'm with my boys we are helping Chloe clean up from the party."*

"You can clean up someone else's house, but I can't get you to clean your room?"

Jordan, *"Can I help finish cleaning up?"*

"No, I want you to come home now. We need to talk to get some things straight."

Jordan sighs, *"Okay I'll be home shortly."*

Vicky, *"Bye."* She then abruptly hangs up the phone.

Jordan puts his phone in his pocket and walks back into the apartment. Nick asks, "Everything good?"

Jordan quietly, "Yeah that was my mom."

Nick asks, "So everything alright?"

Jordan, "Yeah, she still in my shit about last night."

Spenser listening from the kitchen inquires, "So what's up you got to go?

Jordan sigh, "Nah it's cool. She'll be alright let's clean up."

CHAPTER FIVE

Nick pulls up to Jordan's house, Jordan's in the passenger seat, Spenser's in the back asleep. Nick, "Here we are bro I'll get with you later."

Jordan gets out of the car, pulls his phone out to check the time, it's been 2.5 hours since his mother called, she has texted him three different times, he knows he's going to get both barrels from her. He opens the door and she is sitting on the couch working on a jigsaw puzzle. She looks up at him and in a calm voice, "Jordan we need to talk, take a seat."

Jordan unsure about her calm demeanor takes a seat on the couch with some space between them. Vicky, "Look I'm not sure what is going on with you, but we need to get some things straight."

Jordan replies, "What are you talking about?"

Vicky still calm, "Well in the last 24 hours, you went to a party without my permission, you stayed out all night and didn't come home, then you leave your brother here by his self to go with 'your boys,' and when I talk with you on the phone you said you were coming home and don't show up until 2 hours later."

Jordan excited, "Mom I thought I told you about the party and..." Vicky cuts him off tells him to "Calm down, we are having a nice mature conversation. This will go where you take it, you cool I'm cool, just remember that. What were you saying?"

Jordan chuckles, "OK I thought I told you about the party, I didn't come home last night because Nick had been drinking, and I didn't want to wake you up. Today I asked Nick to give me a ride but he stayed to clean up Chloe's house. Did you want me to walk home?"

She looks him in the eyes, "So now we lying to each other? The reason you didn't want to come home is that you were afraid you were going to wake me up? That would not have been a problem at least I know you are safe." She shakes her head up and down like yeah, I believe that. She continues, "We need to come to some kind of understanding today."

Jordan responds, "What does that mean?"

Vicky raises her voice a little, "You are not going to continue to disrespect me in my own house."

Jordan responds and raises his voice, "I'm not trying to disrespect you but stop treating me like a baby."

Vicky's voice still raised, "Look I'm not treating you like a baby, but you're still a child living in my house."

Jordan in a louder voice, "I'm not a child."

Vicky shouts, "You need to watch your tone."

Jordan gets up, "I'm going to my room." He walks out of the living room.

Vicky yells, "I'm not going to be putting up with you disrespecting me in my house too many more times."

Jordan yells, "Okay, Okay I heard you," he slams his bedroom door.

Vicky sits on the couch, and talks to herself to try to remain calm she rocks back and forth mumbles, "Take deep breaths, calm yourself going into his room right now is not going to do anything but make the situation worse." She leans over the coffee table and goes back to working on her puzzle.

Jordan is at the counter of Burger House, it is the middle of the day slowdown between lunch and dinner, and he's bored waiting for some customers to come in. Brittany approaches him at the counter and tells him, "You got some goofy-ass friends."

Jordan's wiping down the counter, "Yeah I know but them my bros." The door opens a boy Jordan doesn't know walks in and behind him is Reign. She is looking at her phone not paying any attention. Her hair is styled differently than it was at the party it has two braid cornrows on each side, she has on a pair of white-rimmed cat-eyed glasses with blue lenses. She has on ripped straight leg blue jeans with a midnight blue cropped daisy floral embroidered tee shirt. The boy is about Jordan's height darker skin, his hair cut in a Mohawk, with twists on top and two half-moon parts on the left side, and a small cross in his left ear. He is wearing a plain white tee shirt with his blue jeans, sagging, listening to music through white headphones.

Jordan seeing her thinks, *Damn she fine, I hope that's her brother,* even though they look nothing alike, he slides the rag over to Brittany and says, "I got this."

Jordan looks directly at Reign in a professional tone says, "Welcome to the Burger House can I take your order?"

She looks up from her phone shocked to see Jordan nervously answers, "Oh yeah, um…

The dude pulls off his headphones looks at Reign annoyed asks, "Yo what's wrong with you? Why you acting all stupid?"

Reign exasperated, "DJ what are you talking about? I'm just trying to think about what I want to order?"

"What?? You ain't new to this. Why you acting sus? Do you know this nigga or something?"

"What are you talking about?" she turns and looks at Jordan and asks, "Do you know me?"

Jordan surprised by the question, "No, I asked her because I saw your headphones and thought you wouldn't hear me."

Dejuan sarcastically responds, "Ok nigga whatever give me a double cheeseburger combo with a sprite," he then puts his headphones back on.

Jordan in his most professional voice turns to Reign, "And what can I get you?" Reign maintaining her cool, "I will have the fish combo with a medium sweet tea."

Jordan asks, "And is that order for here or to go?"

Reign responds, "It's for here."

He punches it in the register, "That's $14.88."

She reaches in her cell phone case and pulls out a single $20 and gives it to him.
Jordan gives her the change. Dejuan turns and walks to a table, Jordan tells Reign, "Your order number is 6."

He gives her a number 6 placard for her table, as she grabs it, he holds on to her hand and looks at her, and gives a wink. She smiles at him and catches up to Dejuan. She taps Dejuan on the shoulder, he pulls down the right-side headphone she tells him, "I need to go to the bathroom."

Brittany watching, laughingly says to Jordan, "He was about to kick yo ass."

Jordan comes back at her, "Don't worry about it mind your own."

Brittany responds, "Yeah okay I'ma check the restrooms to make sure they're clean," and she walks away.

Four minutes later, the cook in the back yells, "Number 6 ready."

Jordan grabs the tray, "I got it."

He walks over to the table. He can hear them arguing Dejuan accusingly asks, "Were you flirting with that fool at the counter?"

"What are you talking about I told you I don't even know him; you need to quit being so jelly."

Jordan approaches the table with their food, Dejuan sees him and sneers, "Now here comes this fool. Really nigga? You don't see us talking?"

Jordan offended, "Yo bro I'm just doing my job; you want your food or not?"

Dejuan yells, "What the fuck you think? We paid for it."

He drops the tray, on the table, some of the fries, spill out of the package onto the tray. Dejuan jumps up, "What the fuck bro?"

Jordan looks him in the eye, "You don't want this smoke you best sit your ass down."

Dejuan meets his gaze. They both are eyeballing one another neither flinching.

Reign grabs on Dejuan's arm pleading, "Come on sit down and eat. I got to get home to babysit my sister."

Dejuan shakes away from Reign, "Let go of me!" He raises his right hand and points it at Jordan's face and threatens him, "Yo nigga you better watch yourself."

He then sits down. Jordan with a smirk on his face slowly nods his head up and down and walks away.

Jordan goes back behind the counter. Brittany hands him a piece of paper Jordan questions, "What's this?"

Brittany says, "Read it."

Jordan opens the paper written on it, *purple Reign 24* on Instagram, and underneath is her phone number *555-1270 hit me up.*

Jordan smiles and folds it back up puts it in his pocket, "Where did you get this?"

Brittany answers, "Your girl came in the bathroom, while I was in there and started telling me about seeing you at a party and how she didn't get a chance to talk with you, but she wants to get to know you. She then gets a paper towel and writes down her number and told me to give it to you."

Ten minutes later Jordan watches as Reign and Dejuan get up and dump their tray. Reign walks by looking straight ahead with Dejuan following closely. He walks by and stares at Jordan, Jordan smiles and says, "Have a nice day."

CHAPTER SIX

Reign walks out the door ahead of Dejuan she turns around and yells, "Hurry up I told you I have to babysit my little sister, my mother has to go to work."

Dejuan gets into the front seat of Reign's red Camaro.

"It's all good I'll just chill with you at your house"

Reign gets into the car and starts it, "Seriously you know I can't have no boy over while my parents are at work."

"Come on girl we don't get a chance to hang out much."

Reign driving says, "Not gonna happen. You want me to drop you off at your house?"

"Nah you can drop me off at the courts. So, you coming through tomorrow?"

"I don't know I have to work tomorrow at one."

Dejuan looks at her and says aggressively, "You sure you not trying to get with that nigga from the store?"

Reign excitedly replies, "What the hell are you talking about? I told you already I don't know him. This jealousy shit is getting old, you need to trust me."

Dejuan excited, "I can't help it every time I see another nigga looking at you, I just get crazy, I love you."

They are stopped at a traffic light Reign looks at Dejuan shocked by that statement replies, "Look I like you, but love that's too much," she shakes her head.

The light turns green she takes off Dejuan ignores her comment answers, "Girl we always going to be together, ain't nobody coming between us."

Reign's phone rings, she pushes the answer button on the steering wheel, "Hello Reign, where you at? I need to get to work."

Reign answers, "Mom I'm about to make the turn to drop DJ off, I should be there in about 15 minutes."

"I'm going to be late because you messing around with some boy."

"I'm sorry I just lost track of time," she turns into the basketball court. "See you in a few minutes." She pushes the hang-up button on the steering wheel.

Dejuan, "What did she mean, 'some boy'? That's all I am is, 'some boy'?"

Reign parks in front of the basketball court, "Really? I don't have time for this you heard her she is about to be late. Get out! I will talk with you later."

Dejuan reaches over to kiss her she turns away and his kiss lands on her right cheek. He is irritated by the move but doesn't say anything. He opens the door gets out and leans down looks at her tells her again, "I love you girl."

Jordan gets into his mother's Camry. KJ and Ericka are in the back seat KJ's wearing earphones plugged into his phone, Ericka is asleep. Jordan, "Thanks for picking me up, I'm sorry you had to wait my manager made me take out the garbage just when I was about to clock out."

"No problem we've all been there when it's time to leave management always finds something else for you to do."

Vicky driving in a cheerful voice, "So how was work today?"

"It was chill," he's thinking about Reign, "I met a girl."

"That's nice so is she a good girl?"

"I didn't get a chance to talk with her too long because of work."

"That's smart you don't want to get into trouble at the job. Did you get her number?"

Jordan smiling answers, "Yeah, I should call her" he pulls out his phone and sees it is 7:40 pm. He thinks *maybe I should wait till later that fool she is with is a punk.*

Jordan puts his phone back in his pocket, "I'll call later."

Vicky, "I need to say something," she pauses for a second, "I want to apologize about the other night, I told you that if you stayed cool that I would, yet I blew up."

Jordan surprised, "Uh it's cool."

"You are the oldest and it can't just be about you hanging out with no responsibilities, I need your help with KJ and Ericka."

Jordan sighs, "OK"

"I know that you just want to be a regular teenager and have fun. It's just sometimes life doesn't always work out how you want it to but that doesn't mean you still can't have fun this summer. Are you hungry?"

"No, I'm good I ate at work. I'm tired I just want to lay down when we get home."

Vicky pulls into the driveway, "Alright we here I'ma run Ericka and KJ to go get something to eat."

Reign is in the kitchen cooking spaghetti, she yells out, "Hey Zoey dinner will be ready in 10 minutes."

Zoey from her room answers, "Good I'm hungry."

Reign asks, "What are you doing?"

"Just playing a game on my phone."

Reign sits down at the table and grabs her phone she texts, Chloe: *Hey what's up with your boy Jordan?* She puts her phone down.

Zoey comes to the kitchen and sits down beside Reign.

Reign, "So let's talk we don't get a chance to anymore." She gets up from the table goes to the stove and stirs the spaghetti, "It should be ready in a few more minutes."

She sits back down at the table asks, "You ready to move?"

Zoey in a low tone answers, "I don't know, I'm miss my friends."

Reign reaches out and touches her hand she smiles, "At least you gonna get a bigger room." Her phone on the table buzzes, "That's probably Chloe," she picks it up it's Dejuan texting: *what's up girl?*

Reign takes a deep breath and says aloud, "Damn he won't give me a second to breathe," she texts back: *I'm making dinner for me and Zoey*, she puts the phone back on the table.

She gets up from the table and goes to the stove grabs a plate, "It's ready." She makes a plate and hands it to Zoey, grabs another plate and fills it up, then sits down, "I wonder what's up with Chloe, she hasn't answered me yet," she picks up her phone it buzzes again it's another text from Dejuan, *you coming through later*

Reign puts the phone down, "Maybe if I don't answer he will catch the hint."

Zoey asks, "Why are you still seeing him?"

She sighs and answers "I don't know when we first started, he was cool, but lately, he's changed, he wants to know where I am and what I'm doing every second of the day."

"So, break up with him."

The phone buzzes again, Reign picks it up and yells, "Damn bro leave me alone." She looks at it, it's a text from Chloe: *He out there, what's up you feeling him?*

Reign texts back: *A little, saw him at Burger House and slipped him my dm for Instagram,* she puts the phone down and continues eating.

Zoey eating asks, "Who's that?"

"It's Chloe. You remember her we played AAU together, she is friends with somebody I'm trying to get to know."

Zoey asks, "So you breaking up with Dejuan?"

"I'm just trying to get to know Jordan, will see where it goes."

Zoey eating tells her, "MMM this is good can I have some more?"

Reign gets up and grabs Zoey's plate "I'm just glad you like it, I don't like cooking, but spaghetti is pretty easy," her phone buzzes she says, "Please don't tell me that's DJ."

Zoey grabs the phone and looks at it and replies, "It's Chloe"

Reign asks, "Can you read it for me?"

I guess if you like that thug lifestyle, Jordan and DJ could be twins.

Reign put some spaghetti on her plate, and sets it down in front of Zoey, "Give me the phone."

She takes the phone from Zoey texts: *hopefully not twins,* she puts the phone down thinks a little bit, picks it back up texts: *Bad boys are more fun,* she laughs to herself a little bit, and puts the phone down.

Her phone buzzes again and she picks it up it's a text from Dejuan: *Why are you ignoring me?*

Reign stares at the phone, mumbles, "I guess he won't catch a hint." She texts back: *I told you I was babysitting, you must trust me if this is going to work,* she puts the phone down and continues to eat.

Dejuan texts back: *I DON'T TRUST NOBODY!*

CHAPTER SEVEN

Vicky knocks on Jordan's bedroom door, she peeks her head in his bedroom, "I'm leaving for work, and KJ is asleep in his room. Do you have to work today?"

Jordan, rolls over and answers, "No, where's Ericka?"

"She stayed overnight with Aunt Shea, she's hanging out with the twins for a girls' day."

Jordan, "Cool Cool, when is she coming home?"

Vicky, "I'm picking her up after work, KJ has a dental appointment at five, so I will be home around four. Be good," she shuts the bedroom door.

A few hours later, KJ knocks on Jordan's bedroom door asks, "You sleep?"

Jordan pulls the blanket over his head, "I was, what's up?"

KJ asks, "You wanna play Madden?"

Jordan laughs, "Seems like we been trying to play Madden forever. Aight let me get up."

"Okay, I'm going to get some Lucky Charms" he shuts the door.

Jordan is in KJ's room, playing Madden, KJ's sitting on his bed, Jordan's is sitting in a desk chair announces, "I'm getting bored we've been playing for over two hours and I have beaten you three straight games."

KJ whines, "Come on let's play one more."

Jordan stands up and stretches his arm above his head with the controller in his right hand he throws it on the bed and laughs, "You play the computer you need the practice," he walks out the room, "I need to check my phone to see what's going on."

Jordan goes to his room and grabs his phone off his desk, thinks to himself *I wonder if I should slide into Reign's dm, it's too early for her to be with that nigga.*

He finds his work pants on the floor goes through the pockets and finds her note, looks at it, looks at his phone, it's 11:30 am he thinks, *What the hell.* He dm's her: *What's up I'm sorry about not getting with you sooner, just trying not to cause you any drama with that fool.*

He looks at his phone and sees he has a text message from Spenser: *Yo fool, you want to go to the park and ball?*

The text was sent fifteen minutes ago.

Jordan texts back: *cool my lil bro has to come, give me 20 minutes to get ready.*

Jordan shouts, "KJ we about to go ball so get ready."

KJ excitedly asks, "Ok, can I asks Dre if he wants to play?"

Jordan yells back, "I don't care, he has to get his own ride out there."

"I'm texting him right now."

"Alright, get ready, they coming by in about 20 minutes."

Twenty-seven minutes later, Nick pulls into Jordan's driveway and blows the horn.

Jordan yells to KJ he's in the bathroom, "Yo Nick's here let's go."

KJ flushes the toilet opens the door, "Aight let's go."

Jordan playfully pushes KJ as he leaves the bathroom, and walks down the hall. KJ walks out of the house as Jordan locks the door. KJ and Jordan jump in the backseat of Nick's car.

Spenser turns around as Nick takes off to greet them, "What up J, lil, J."

Jordan laughs, "It's all good."

KJ with a serious look and tone, "I ain't little J, I'm KJ."

Spenser laughs him off, "Chill little J."

Nick driving asks, "So J, what's been up?"

"Yesterday Reign came through the job with her man, that fool is stupid."

Spenser asks, "So what happened?"

"He got salty and accused her of flirting with me."

Nick asks, "Well, was she?"

43

Jordan laughs, "Well maybe, she lied and said she didn't know me, I don't know why she's with him. Check this he stepped to me while I was at work."

Spenser turns around from the front and exclaims, "Really!! So what happened?"

Jordan responds, "What do you think happened? I came back at him, and he chilled the fuck out."

Nick turns into the basketball courts. Spenser laughs, "Yo I guess you let him know what's up."

Jordan laughs, "And I still got her Insta gram tag."

Nick parks the car in front of the courts, it is two full basketball courts with chain nets. There is a group of boys, running a full-court game on the court farthest away from the parking lot. At the near court is 2 boys, KJ 's age shooting around, KJ jumps out of the car, "There's Dre and Cage," he runs to the court.

They then get out of the car, Nick shuts the driver's door and inquires, "How did you pull that off?"

"She gave it to Brittany in the bathroom."

All three laugh, as they walk to the trunk, Nick hits the clicker, Spenser gets the basketball out of the trunk. He dribbles the ball to the court he simply says, "You the man J."

CHAPTER EIGHT

Vicky gets in her Camry pushes the phone button on the dashboard and calls Shea her sister in law, the phone rings three times, Vicky talking loudly, "What's up girl, I just call to let you know I'm off and, on the way, to pick up Ericka."

Shea, "Alright we're here, just watching TV"

"Ok, I should be there in fifteen minutes or so, depending on the traffic."

Shea "Ok, she'll be ready when you get here."

"Great, see you soon."

Shea "Bye."

Vicky continues driving pushes the phone again yells, "Call Jordan" the phone rings eight times and goes to voice mail, she hangs up. "I need him to have KJ ready for this appointment," she says loudly out of frustration.

Jordan, KJ, Spenser, and Nick are sitting on the sideline, Dre and Cage are playing horse. Jordan is looking at the boys on the other court playing and sees one of them is Dejuan. Jordan reaches around KJ and pushes Spenser on his left shoulder, "I don't believe this shit, see that nigga in the white shorts and blue t-shirt, that's Dejuan."

Spenser looks over at him and asks, "Who?"

45

Jordan points "That fool I was talking about on the way over, Reign's nigga."

Nick laughing, "Yo really?"

Jordan "No shit, I need to hit her up, now that I know that her nigga ain't all up in her face."

Nick confirms, "Yeah you should."

KJ's bored and gets up walks to the court where Dre and Cage are playing horse, "Yo can I get in the next game?"

The game across the court is over, Dejuan's team won, the losing team walks off the court, Tristan a bro they know grabs a black gym bag puts it on his left shoulder and walks toward them.

Spenser knows Tristan sells weed and he asks Jordan and Nick, "Yo do y'all want to get some smoke?"

Jordan surprised by the question, "What? Fool I got my lil bro here."

Spenser points at the court, "Chill bro, he ain't paying no attention to us he's ballin."

Nick, "We will do it in my car he won't see anything."

Spenser signals for Tristan to come over, Tristan walks over, looks down at Spenser asks, "Yo what's up?"

Spenser replies, "You holding anything?"

Tristan, "Yeah I got something. What you want?" He drops his bag by Spenser.

"Woo hold up we can do this in the car."

Tristan picks his bag up, "Say no mo."

Spenser, Nick, and Jordan stand up and walk to the car with Tristan following behind, Nick gets in the driver's side with Spenser in the front seat and Jordan in the passenger seat behind Nick.

Tristan stops at the driver's door, stoops down looks in the car, "So what you want?"

Nick looking around the car says, "Both of y'all put in 20 each so we can get 4 grams"

Jordan asks, "What about you?"

Nick loudly, "Who ride you in?"

Spenser laughs and hands, Nick, a $20. Jordan "Aight", he pulls his wallet out the door storage bin. He pulls $20 out of his wallet and gives it to Nick.

Tristan reaches in his gym bag and pulls out a clear zip-lock bag, "This is some of that OG Kush."

Nick reaches for the baggie Tristan pulls it back, "Straight cash homie."

Nick, "Yo dog relax" as he hands him the money.

Tristan gives him the weed and throws the money in his gym bag as he stands up, "Later bro" he walks away towards his green ford focus.

Spenser confidently, "Let's fire it up."

Jordan, "You for real my lil bro is on the court."

Spenser, "Damn would you chill bro he ballin he ain't worried about you."

Jordan, "Aight maybe one, but hurry up."

Nick closes the window, says to Spenser, "Get the papers out of the glove box."

Spenser leans over and opens the glove box, there is a gun inside of it, he picks it up and holds it in front of his face, "What are you doing with a gun?"

"You never know what or who you might run into it's best to be prepared."

Jordan taps Spenser on the shoulder, "Let me get it."

Spenser holds the gun and looks at it as he passes it back over his head to Jordan, Jordan grabs it, "Where's the mag at?"

Nick opens the center console and pulls out the magazine, "I keep it unloaded I'm not trying to be a statistic because fools like to pretend, they hard."

Jordan holds the gun, looks through the sights out the other passenger window.

Nick turns around and tells him, "Alright you had your fun, now put it back before someone sees you."

Jordan hands the gun back to Spenser and he puts it back in the glove box then he pulls out a pack of raw papers.

Nick grabs the pack leans over the center storage bin and rolls a joint, holding it up, smiling says, "Back in the zoot box." Jordan hands him his lighter from the backseat.

Spenser pulls his phone from the door storage bin, checks it out, and sees that Reign left an Instagram dm: *Sorry I'm at work, will get back to you after I get off.*

Vicky pulls into Shea's, driveway, rings the doorbell, a female voice inside the house asks, "Who is it?"

Vicky responds, "It's Vicky, your favorite sister-in-law."

Shea opens the door she is 5'11" light-skinned with sleek straighten jet black shoulder-length hair. She has on very little make-up, she's wearing a pair of high-waisted jeans and a shamrock green t-shirt with a dandelion flower imprint in the center.

Vicky laughs, Shea opens the door all the way, "Come on in."

Vicky steps into the house, they hug, "I can't stay long, gotta get KJ to his dental appointment."

Shea asks, "So how's it going?"

Vicky breathes deeply and answers, "In a word tense."

Shea concerned, "What's going on?"

Vicky, "Jordan's out here in the streets, thinking he's grown staying out all night." Vicky chuckles a little, "I wish I would have had all girls."

Shea laughs back, "You say that but girls ain't no walk in the park either. You ever thought about getting his father back into his life?"

Vicky takes a deep breath, "I don't know I ain't sure, he hasn't always been the best role model."

Shea, "Well he is his father, maybe it's time for him to step up."

Vicky changes the subject, "So where are the twins?"

Shea, "They are at cheerleading camp."

Vicky, "Where is Ericka? I haven't heard a word from her."

Shea answers, "She was watching TV in one of the twin's rooms. I think she fell asleep, I'll go get her."

Shea walks out, Vicky pulls out her phone and looks at it, and checks it for messages. Nothing.

Shea comes back out with Ericka behind her, Shea steps to the right and yells, "Tada" holding her hands out towards Ericka. Ericka is coca brown 4'10" she is wearing some dark blue leggings and a light blue t-shirt that says Best Sister Ever in pink and white letters. She has a brand-new hairstyle her hair is braided together on the sides then tied all together with one long ponytail down the center just past her shoulders.

Vicky walks up and puts her hands on her shoulders spins her round, mouth open gasping says, "This is gorgeous, I love it." Ericka is spinning around showing it off.

Shea "I'm glad you like it."

Vicky looks at Ericka asks, "You like it?"

Ericka laughs, "This is the best hairstyle I ever had in my whole life."

Vicky looks at Shea, "Thank you, what do I owe you?"

Shea "Girl we good, it's a late birthday present since I forgot it last month."

Ericka looks at Shea, "You're my favorite aunt."

Shea hugs her, "Thank you, sweetie."

Vicky to Ericka, "We need to go so we can get KJ to his appointment."

Ericka turns to Shea smiling says, "Bye and thank you for my birthday present."

Shea opens the door, Vicky lets Ericka get in front of her and walks out behind her. They walk to the car she turns around waves and yells, "Tell Antonio and the twins I said hi," as she gets in the car.

Vicky starts the car, tells Ericka "I tried calling Jordan earlier and he didn't answer, I hope everything is alright," she pushes the phone button on her car dashboard.

CHAPTER NINE

"Dear Mama" plays on Jordan's phone as it sits on the back seat. He picks it up looks at it and puts it back on the seat. He takes a hit of the joint and passes it to Nick.

Spencer laughing says, "Bro what's up with this song? You need to change it."

Jordan snaps at him, "Shut Up," and answers the phone, *"Hello."*

Vicky in a loud voice, *"How come you didn't pick up the phone when I called? Where you at? Is KJ with you?"*

Jordan in a calm voice, *"Mom calm down, me and KJ are at the park playing ball."*

Vicky calming down, *"Ok I just get nervous. Have you forgot that KJ has a dental appointment at five?"*

Jordan pulls the phone away from his ear and looks at the time it's 3:50, *"Um yeah I kinda did forget."*

"Well I'm just pulling into the driveway, you need to get home, we can still make it to the appointment, I need you to watch Ericka."

Jordan hearing this ask, *"Can't she just go with you to KJ's appointment?"*

"She said she didn't want to go besides, it will give you the chance to show that I can trust you. Look

you need to be headed home so we can make this appointment. Bye."

Jordan drops his phone on the seat, "Damn I forgot all about the dentist appointment, she is going to flip the hell out if we show up smelling like weed."

Nick and Spenser laugh, Nick still laughing says, "Yo bro I feel for you, so what you gonna do?"

Spenser takes another hit of the joint and passes it back to Jordan, Jordan slaps his hand away, "Fool are you serious?"

Spenser laughs, "My bad."

"Roll the window down, let's get some air in here."

Nick starts the car and lets the windows down. Jordan opens the back-car door, steps out, and yells to KJ, "Come on we have to go you got a dentist appointment."

KJ looks at him yells, "Aight let me hit this last jumper."

He shoots the ball from the top of the key and it is an air ball, Dre gets the rebound, KJ, "One more shot." He shoots again it hits the front of the rim.

Jordan yells at KJ, "Come on fool, we gotta go, mom is already pissed."

KJ, "I'm coming" he shoots the ball again nothing but net he sprints off the court and runs to the driver's side back door.

KJ jumps in the back seat, the car is filled with weed smoke, Jordan gets back in the car and shuts the door, "Let's go."

KJ starts coughing as he sits in the car, he looks at Jordan, "You smoke weed?" Nick backs out and starts driving.

Jordan snaps at him, "Don't worry about it."

Spenser holds up the burnout end of the joint and offers it to KJ, "You want to hit it?"

Jordan smacks him in the back of the head, "Yo fool quit fucking around, my mom is already going to jump my ass, I just hope the smell is gone before we get home."

Spenser turns around and flicks the joint out the window, Jordan tells him, "Keep the windows down so we can air it out."

Nick driving after about three minutes says, "That's enough," rolls the window's up, "It's too hot to have the windows down I'm turning on the a/c, he pulls the weed from the door pocket and hands it to Spenser, "Put this in the glove box."

Spenser puts it in the glove box, next to the gun, says loudly, "Damn Nick, weed, a gun, you a regular g."

Nick continues driving, shakes his head tells him, "Shut up fool."

Jordan asks, "You got any eye drops, mouthwash something?"

Nick replies, "Nah man sorry."

"Damn I wished I wouldn't forgot about that appointment," he looks at KJ, "Why didn't you say something?"

KJ answers, "I forgot too, I didn't know you were going to smoke weed."

Jordan sighs, "What's done is done."

Jordan's phone buzzes he looks at it's a text message from Reign: *You at work? I'm about to get off I can stop by and see you.*

Jordan chuckles to himself, "Damn the one time I wish I was at work."

Nick asks, "Why?? What's up?"

Jordan, "Reign just hit me up. She was getting off work and was gonna stop by."

Jordan answers back, *No I'm off today, I have something going on I will get with you later."* He turns his camera on looks at himself in selfie mode and, sees his droopy bloodshot eyes, thinks *damn I look high he* shakes his head and puts his phone back in his pocket.

Spenser turns around looks at Jordan, "The way your mom is going to go off on you, you won't see her for at least a year."

Jordan replies, "Damn bro how do you always manage to say the wrong thing?"

KJ replies, "Well mom is going to be mad."

Jordan, "Alright tell me something I don't know."

Nick pulls up to Jordan's house, "We here dog."

Jordan takes a deep breath, opens the door tells KJ, "Let's go."

CHAPTER TEN

Jordan walks to the front door, with KJ behind him, he unlocks the door, Vicky's in the kitchen yells to KJ, "You need to hurry up and change out them sweaty clothes, we got less than an hour, to get to your appointment, and with traffic, it will probably take the full hour."

Ericka's on the couch watching TV asks, "What's that funny smell?"

KJ yells, "OK" as he walks to his room.

Jordan goes to his room and shuts his door, Vicky walks from the kitchen to Jordan's room she opens the door and sticks her head in, he is lying down on the bed she tells him, "Ericka doesn't want to go you need to watch her."

Vicky walks into the room, sniffs the air, and walks to Jordan who is lying with his back turned to her asks, "Is that weed I smell?"

Jordan without turning around answers, "No. I don't know what you are talking about."

Vicky says louder, "Boy turn around and look at me when I'm talking to you."

Jordan turns around and faces her his eyes are glazed up and red bloodshot his clothes reeking of weed.

Vicky yells, "You been smoking weed with KJ? What the hell is wrong with you??"

Jordan sits up and yells back, "That's not what happened, Nick and Spenser were smoking and I was in the car but I wasn't smoking, KJ wasn't in the car he was playing basketball."

Ericka and KJ hear the yelling and walk to the room and stand outside the door, Ericka asks, "What's going on? Why are you yelling at Jordan?"

Vicky looks at Ericka, "I'm sorry for being so loud it's just that your brother did something really, really stupid today with KJ, go back in the living room, everything is ok."

Ericka looks in the room at Jordan sitting on the bed, he stares straight ahead she smiles at him and walks away.

Vicky walks into the room sits on the bed beside Jordan says in a lower voice, "You expect me to believe that you were in the car and didn't smoke anything? How stupid do you think I am? Look at you, your eyes are all red and glassy and you smell like you been hanging with Snoop Dogg."

"I'm telling you mama I didn't smoke anything."

Vicky shakes her head, "You must think I'm a fool because you keep thinking I'm going to believe your lies."

KJ is still standing at the door when Vicky looks at him tells him, "Come here," motioning with her hand for him to come into the room.

KJ walks into the room, "What momma?" she grabs him by his arm and pulls him close, she looks directly at him, "I want you to tell me the truth."

KJ looks at her nervously, "Ok."

"Did Jordan smoke weed with you?"

"No, I was playing basketball with Dre and Cage."

"You not lying to protect Jordan, are you?"

"No momma, I swear I didn't know nothing about them smoking I was playing basketball."

"So, you don't know if Jordan smoked any?"

KJ shakes his head no.

Vicky stares at him for a few seconds trying to see if he is lying, tells him, "Go to your room brush your teeth, and change, you smell like it too."

KJ walks out of the room. Jordan feels vindicated, "See I told you."

Vicky stands up and looks down at him, "You think this is over? After the talk we had a few days ago you still doing dumb stuff, exposing your little brother to weed, he might not have smoked any but I ain't no fool I know you smoked. KJ looks up to you, you are only thinking about yourself. I got to get KJ to the dentist."

She walks to the door, Jordan says, "I don't know why you making such a big deal about it was only weed."

Vicky surprised by the statement turns around looks at him, "Only weed? That's it! I'm tired of your disrespect, I gotta get KJ to the dentist, but here is something for you to think about, they say the definition of insanity is to keep doing the same thing and expect a different result and I ain't crazy."

Jordan confused asks, "What does that mean?"

"You'll find out." She walks out of the room and shuts the door.

CHAPTER ELEVEN

Jordan gets up out of his bed, opens the bedroom and door walks to the kitchen he goes to the fridge asks, "We got anything to eat?" Ericka is still lying on the couch watching TV does not answer.

Jordan grabs a package of Oreo cookies, goes to the couch, and sits down at the end of Ericka's feet, "Is momma and KJ back yet?"

Ericka answers, "No," she sits up and looks at Jordan, "Why was momma yelling at you?"

Jordan a little surprised by the question answers, "She doesn't like my friends."

"Do you smoke weed?"

Jordan chuckles, "What do you know about weed?"

Ericka laugh, "My dad smokes weed, I've seen Friday. So, do you like smoking it?"

Jordan thinks for a few seconds, "I don't know, I was hanging out with Nick, then he started running with Spenser, and he smoked weed so we both tried it, I wish I would have never started."

Ericka "So why don't you quit?"

"It's not that easy," he gets up off the couch and states, "I gotta use the bathroom." On the way back to the living room he stops by his room and gets his phone, he sits back down on the couch looks at it, and sees that Reign has hit him up on Instagram. *So, what's up??*

Jordan: *At home babysitting my lil sis Ericka*

Reign answers back: *I'm doing the same thing too.*

Jordan smiles thinking about the coincidence: *What's her name, how old is she?*

Reign: *Zoey and she is 9. What about yours?*

Jordan: *Ericka and she is 9, they have to meet.*

Reign: *Cool, so what are you doing tomorrow?*

Jordan: *Work, I get off at 10.*

Reign: *Well that's late, will have to get them together another time, maybe I can come through while you're at work.*

Jordan: *Cool, what about your man? I saw him at the courts today.*

Reign: *Did he say anything to you?*

Jordan: *No, he didn't see me.*

Reign: *I'm cutting him loose; he is getting too intense.*

Jordan: *When?*

Reign: *Probably tomorrow before I come to see you.*

Jordan: *How do you think he is going to take it?*

Reign: *Don't know not good.*

Jordan: *I got you.*

Reign: *Thanks, later.*

Vicky sits in the waiting room, while KJ is in the exam room with the dentist. She gets on her phone, goes through her contacts, pushes the dial button, the phone rings six times.

"This is Keith what's up?"

"Keith this is your ex, I'm calling because we have a problem."

'We?' We don't have anything, you let me know that last time I came by."

"Look it's time you stepped up and be a dad to Jordan."

"What are you talking about?"

"Jordan, he is out of control, going out to parties, staying out all night, and today he was smoking weed with KJ."

"So why are you telling me all this?"

"I'm telling you this because it's time you stepped up and be a dad to your son. He can live with you for a while."

"WHAT?" Hold up, you talking about him moving in with me?"

"Why not you his father, time for you to act like it."

"Woo, slow down you dropping all this on me, right now."

"It's either with you or in the streets, he crossed the line, when he brought KJ into his thug ways, look maybe you can reach him, right now I'm lost."

Keith sighs, "Ok, Ok I can't turn my back on my son. How long are we talking, and how soon?"

"Since school is out, at least the rest of the summer, and I'm dropping him off tomorrow after he gets off work."

"Tomorrow?' I only have a 1-bedroom apartment, I have to go shopping I am not ready."

"You got the rest of today and all day tomorrow to get ready."

"You are putting me in a bad spot."

"I have been there for 16 years, now it's your turn."

KJ walks out to the dentist waiting room with the dental receptionist behind him he has one of the sample bags with a toothbrush and toothpaste in them.

Vicky "I got to go I will talk to you tomorrow." She pushes the hang-up button.

CHAPTER TWELVE

Jordan is on the fryer dumping the fries in the basket, his manager Mark, comes up behind him and tells him, "You can take a break in 15 minutes."

Jordan turns around looks at him, "Thanks, Mark."

He turns and asks Vince, "Yo can you watch this? I got to use the bathroom."

Vince walks over to the fryer, "Just make sure you watch your hands."

Jordan walking away chuckles, "Come on bro."

He walks to the bathroom and goes into the stall pulls out his phone, texts Reign: *I got a break in 15 minutes hope you can come through.* Puts his phone in his pocket then uses the bathroom.

He goes to the sink, turns on the water, and laughs to himself thinking about Vince's comment.

He walks out, sees Mark, and asks him, "Since it's slow is it cool if I just go on break now?"

Mark looks at the empty store answers, "Sure go ahead, and don't forget to clock out."

Jordan goes clock out and grabs a soda and takes a seat in the restaurant, he pulls his phone out and goes to the chess game he is playing online.

Brittany's wiping down the tables comes up to Jordan asks him, "So what's with that girl who slid you her Instagram?"

"We still feeling each other out."

"So, what about her boyfriend?"

Jordan defensively a little louder, "What about him?"

"I was just asking, I saw how he stepped to you last time he was here."

Jordan shakes his head, "He don't want this smoke."

Reign and a little girl come into the restaurant Brittany leans down and whispers into Jordan's right ear, "Here comes trouble." Jordan playfully pushes her away and tells her, "Go somewhere."

Reign and the girl sit down at the table. Jordan looks at Reign, "Wow, I'm shocked when I didn't hear back from you, I didn't think you were gonna make it."

Reign replies, "Me and Zoey were out running some errands, I thought I would surprise you."

Jordan looks at Zoey, "What's up nice to meet you, I got a lil sis Ericka that's about your age."

Reign tells Zoey, "This is my friend Jordan."

Zoey looks at Jordan asks, "Are you my sister's new boyfriend?"

Reign looks at her surprised and laughs, "I'm sorry I know that was inappropriate."

Jordan laughs replies, "She just goes straight for the gut."

Zoey looks at Reign, "Well I know you don't like DJ anymore and we are here talking to him."

"Slow down, one thing at a time, we are just friends getting to know each other."

Jordan decides to put Zoey on the spot and asks, "Would you like for me to be her new boyfriend?"

Zoey pauses answers, "I don't know... yeah maybe."

Jordan looks at Reign, "I would like that too. So, have you talked with Dejuan?"

Reign, "I haven't had a chance, I'm going by his house and talk with him tonight."

A voice behind the counter yells out, "Jordan your break is over, let's go," he looks back it's his manager Mark.

Jordan stands up and replies, "Cool." All three of them are standing up, he looks at Reign, "I got to get back to work," he goes in for a kiss, she puts her hand up to stop him saying, "We ain't there yet," she hugs him. Jordan turns to Zoey tells her, "I'll be seeing you around."

Vicky is waiting outside in the car for Jordan to get off work, she puts the car in park, turns the radio to the quiet storm, lets the seat back, closes her eyes, the song, "Wait For Love" by Luther Vandross is playing. After 15 minutes Jordan comes out and jumps in the front seat.

He startles her out of her comfort zone.

"What's up mom were you asleep?"

Vicky sits up and adjusts the seat, "No I was just resting my eyes," she starts the car.

Jordan looks in the backseat inquires, "Where's Ericka and KJ?"

Vicky looks over at Jordan, "That's what we need to talk about, Ericka is over at Antonio's and Shea's and KJ is staying the night with Dre."

Jordan nervously, "What's going on?"

"I wanted them both out of the house because I did not want to upset them. I'm just gonna tell it to you straight, I'm taking you to live with your father."

Jordan shocked, "Are you serious? Why?"

"You got some nerve asking me 'why' after your behavior in the last week, you crossed the line when you smoked weed with KJ. How am I supposed to trust you?"

Jordan "I already told you, that I didn't smoke, I don't know why you don't believe me."

Vicky does not respond, she continues to drive, Jordan just sits there in the front seat pouting. Vicky pushes the phone button on her car dashboard the phone rings Keith answers, Vicky over the speakerphone, "We should be there in less than 10 minutes. "

Keith replies, "No problem I'm here."

Vicky says, "See you then," she hangs up the phone. Jordan looks over and asks her, "So how long I'm staying there?"

"I'm not sure, will see how this goes."

Vicky turns into The Gardens luxury apartment complex pulls up to the security gate lets her window down she pushes the intercom button. "We out here."

The gate opens, she drives through, the complex has just recently opened it is a resort-style luxury apartment. Driving past the fitness center and pool, she makes a left and pulls into a covered parking spot. She looks at Jordan tells him, "You know there is a scene at the beginning of the movie Boyz in the Hood, where Tre's mom is dropping him off to live with his dad? After she drops him off, she tells Furious, 'I can't teach him how to be a man that's your job.' I think we have reached that point here." She turns and opens the car door, and tells Jordan, "Come on get your bag out of the trunk."

CHAPTER THIRTEEN

Reign is waiting outside Dejuan's apartment at Hills Point she blows the horn DJ comes out and jumps in the front seat, kisses her on the right cheek, and asks, "What's up girl? I ain't heard from you all day."

"Well I've just been busy lately with work, practice, and watching Zoey," she replies.

Dejuan asks, "Yo can you run me to the store? Our car is in the shop."

"Sure, I can get some gas while you are shopping."

"I ain't shopping, I'm just picking up some stuff"

"Okay. I didn't mean anything by it."

Dejuan turns on the radio, Chris Brown's "No Guidance" is playing, and he leans back and rocks with the beat.

Dejuan looks at Reign and asks, "So when are we going to get the chance to chill?"

"I don't know, actually there is something I need to tell you?"

"What's up?"

Dejuan's phone rings, he pulls it out of his pocket, answers, "What's up Dez?"

Dez on the phone, "Momma wants you to pick up some laundry soap too."

Dejuan "Aight cool," he hangs up.

Reign has already pulled into the parking lot. She drives up to the front to let Dejuan out. "I'm going to get some gas I'll be back in a few."

Dejuan replies, "Cool," as he gets out of the car.

Jordan Vicky and Keith are in his apartment, Vicky and Keith sit on the couch, with Jordan sitting on a recliner facing them.

Vicky looks at Jordan, "This is not a punishment, your behavior is stressing me out, and I have KJ and Ericka at home, you need to think about how your behavior is influencing them."

Keith on the couch leaning forward with his elbows on his knees looks at Jordan, "Look son, me and your mother talked and we both agree that maybe it's best if you move in with me for a while."

"What choice do I have?"

"None, we just want what is best for you. Besides, it will give us a chance to get to know each other better."

Jordan sighs and stands up, "Whatever. Where is the bathroom?"

Keith stands up and points, "Go down the hall, my room is on the right the bathroom is on the left."

When Jordan walks away, Keith sits back down Vicky looks at him, "So what do you think?"

"I don't know, I guess will have to wait and see."

Vicky stands up, "Well I guess I should be going."

Keith stands up, "I'll walk you to your car."

"Ok", she grabs her purse, Keith follows behind her and opens the door for her. She gets to the car door clicks it unlock she turns around. Keith is right there behind her.

"I just want to say thank you," she says.

Keith steps closer towards her. "Well he is my son too I want to be there to hopefully prevent him from making the same mistakes I made."

"I see you don't learn from your mistakes."

He walks even closer and presses up against her pushing her into the car door. Keith leans down and moves into a kiss, "Was it really a mistake?" he kisses her, tongue and all.

Vicky kisses him back, after a few seconds she pulls away, "I didn't want this to happen."

"It's cool, no pressure, like with Jordan we will wait and see."

Vicky smiles, turns around, opens the car door, "Goodnight Keith."

Reign parks in front of Dejuan's apartment. "We're here."

He asks, "Can you help with the bags?"

Reign pauses a moment answers, 'Yeah sure," she gets out of the car at the same time as Dejuan they go to the trunk, she clicks it open and there are between 7-10 plastic grocery bags.

He grabs a few of them, she grabs the rest. There is a big bottle of laundry detergent that's left in the trunk.

Dejuan walks away and says, "I'll come back and get that." Reign follows behind him.

Dejuan kicks on the front door and a boy around 12 or 13 years old opens the door. It's his younger brother Dezera. Dejuan yells, "Move fool" and the boy quickly gets out of the way.

Dejuan walks quickly through the living room with Reign following him into the kitchen.

Dejuan tells Reign, "I'm going get the detergent, you can stay and chill on the couch."

She answers back, "I will come with you."

They walk out to the trunk; Dejuan grabs the detergent. Reign, "Like I was saying earlier I need to tell you something."

"Ok, what's up?"

Reign looking up at DJ takes a deep breath, "There ain't no easy way to say this, I think we need to break up."

Dejuan drops the detergent back in the trunk, yells, "WHAT? WHY?"

Reign looks down at the ground. "Your jelly is driving me crazy. After we got together it got even worse."

Dejuan breathes heavily sneers. "It's that nigga from Burger House, ever since we ate there you been acting sus."

Reign looks up at Dejuan. 'Sus?' "You text me all day asking me what am I doing? Where I'm at? I just need some space." She grabs his detergent and shoves it in his chest. "Here take this so I can go."

Dejuan grabs her by her shoulders and looks her straight in her face. "We will never be broken up!" He snatches the detergent out of her hand and walks to his apartment.

CHAPTER FOURTEEN

Keith comes back into the apartment. Jordan is back in the recliner. Keith takes a seat on the couch, grabs a cigar from the coffee table and lights it up takes a big puff. "You don't mind, do you?"

Jordan just shrugs his shoulders. Keith continues, "So what's been up with you? Talk to me."

Jordan quietly, "I don't know. I'm glad school is out, I got a job at Burger House, I chill with my bros."

Keith asks, "Are these the same bros you smoke weed with?"

"Like I told mom I don't smoke weed with them."

"Whatever. I don't care about that, it's one thing if you smoke weed with your friends, but I do agree with your mom, smoking with KJ around is showing a bad example."

Keith takes another puff off the cigar, "You got a girlfriend?"

Jordan has a small smile come across his face, "I am trying to get to know this one girl I met at work."

Keith hears this laughs, "Okay, okay so what's her name?"

"It's Reign. We're just getting to know each other."

Keith takes one long puff off the cigar. "Aight I know how that goes. Is that who you were on the phone with?"

"No, I was just playing my online chess game."

"So, you play chess?"

"Yeah, I ain't too good. Still learning the game."

Keith puts the cigar out in the ashtray. "I play myself. We gonna have to get a game going."

Jordan is unsure. "I don't know I'm still learning. Is it cool if I text Reign about me living here now?"

Keith shakes his head in agreement. "Sure, I would even like to meet her."

Jordan looks at his phone and says, "Ok will see."

Reign pulls into the driveway and parks in the garage. She gets out of her car, and as she walks through the laundry room to the kitchen, her phone dings it's a text from Chloe: *you going to play summer ball. Practice starts in a few weeks.*

She hears her dad in their bedroom. "Dad am I going to be able to play ball this summer?"

A man's voice yells back, "You should just want to get this move done and over with."

Reign hollers back, "So when exactly are we moving?"

He yells back, "I have to go out of town next week for work, and I still waiting for the VA to approve the loan."

"So, what should I tell Chloe about playing ball?"

He responds, "Just tell her to save you a spot, you might not be there for the start."

Reign picking up her phone texts: *save my spot.* She then drops the phone on the bed, then she plops down backward on the bed.

Her phone buzzes again. Still laying down she feels for her phone. When she finds it and lifts it above her head it's a dm from Jordan: *my mom kicked me out of the house, living with my dad.*

She immediately sits up and hits the call button.

Jordan's phone rings he gets up and walks out the front door, *"I didn't know you would call me."*

"So, what happened?"

Jordan explains, *"Me and my mom have been arguing a lot lately, she says she is getting tired of me and kicked me out to go live with my dad."*

"That's it?"

Jordan responds, *"Basically, I'm just sitting here my dad is at work man it feels funny saying that."*

Reign asks, *"So how is that going?"*

Jordan admits, *"So far it's cool, last night was the first night. Did you talk with what's his name?"*

"You mean DJ? Yeah, I did."

Jordan asks, *"So how did he take it?"*

Reign sighs, *"Not too good, he said we will never be broken up."*

Jordan complains, *"That nigga's gonna be a problem."*

Reign says, *"Yeah, I know."*

"You scared?"

"A little, I don't know what he will do."

Jordan, *"Look girl I got you, we in this together. So, when we play that game you promised me?"*

Reign is confused, *"What?"*

Jordan reminds her, *"That night at Chloe's party when we first met."*

"Oh yeah, I forgot between work, babysitting my sister, and packing to move I don't know when I'll have the time."

Jordan teasingly, *"Sounds like someone making excuses because they scared."*

Reign retorts, *"Say less, I gotta work this weekend but I'm off Monday. We can do it then if you ain't scared."*

"I got to close Monday, but we can do it that morning."

"Alright you on, I got to go, talk to you later."

CHAPTER FIFTEEN

Monday morning, Dejuan's wearing his headphones knocks on Tristan's apartment door. Tristan opens the door and says, "Yo what's up?"

Dejuan asks, "Can I get a ride over to my girl Reign's house?"

Tristan shrugs his shoulder. "Yeah cool, let me get my keys." He walks down the hall to his bedroom. Dejuan steps into the apartment and pulls his phone out of his pocket and calls Reign it rings 3 times and goes to voice mail. He hangs it up and squeezes his phone then puts it in his back pocket.

"Alright let's go. So why you need a ride?"

Dejuan explains, "She is not answering her phone just making sure everything is good."

Tristan opens the door, Dejuan follows behind him. He opens the driver's door and pops the lock for the passenger door.

"Get in."

Dejuan jumps in the front seat. Tristan starts the car and backs out of the parking spot, Tristan asks, "Which way?"

Dejuan answers, "Just head towards the school."

"Cool."

Dejuan asks, "You got anything to smoke?"

"You got any cash?"

Dejuan replies, "I ain't got anything on me right now, you know I'm good for it."

Tristan driving explains, "It don't work like that DJ. That's just not good business."

"Whatever bro."

Tristan continues, "The school is up on the left. Which way?"

"Once you get past the school make a right on the next street."

"Then what?"

Dejuan instructs, "Keep straight till I tell you to turn." He pulls his phone out again and calls Reign once again the phone rings 3 times and goes to voice mail. He hangs up and slams the side of his fist on the dashboard and yells, "Why won't she answer her damn phone."

Tristan yells back, "What the hell is wrong with you? Don't take your problems out on my car."

Dejuan looks at Tristan and in a low threatening tone says, "Don't talk to me."

Reign, Zoey Jordan, and Ericka are at the Hill Point basketball court, Zoey and Ericka are at the half-court circle messing around on their phone. Reign and Jordan are playing a game of horse. Reign hears her phone ringing on the sideline, she runs to pick it and up looks at the screen yells, "Damn this is the 5th time DJ has called me in the last two hours."

Jordan's at the free throw line stops dribbling turns towards her. "Why don't you put your phone on silent?"

Reign explains, "I need it turned up in case my mom calls."

Jordan asks, "What if you just talk to him?"

Reign laughs a little and shakes her head no, "I don't think that would work."

Jordan suggests, "Block him."

"Sure, why not." She then starts messing with her phone, after one minute. "Done," she takes her phone up to Zoey, "Hold this," as she hands her the phone.

Jordan turns around asks Zoey, "What time is it?"

Zoey looks at the phone yells, "Two fifteen."

"Damn I didn't realize it was that late I got to be at work at three. We got to drop Ericka off, I need to take a shower, and I'm need a ride to work."

Reign replies, "So, I'm going to have to drop Ericka off. Then run you to your dad's, then take you to work? What if I say no?"

"No! Why would you say no? Just drop Ericka off, I got a uniform at the house. Come on let's go" He jogs to the car.

Reign pulls up to the front of Jordan's house he opens the car door and lifts the seat and Ericka jumps out, she tells Zoey, "It was fun. See you around."

Zoey answers, "Okay. Hope to see you soon."

Ericka runs to the house. Jordan looks through the car door at Reign. "Give me ten minutes."

Reign agrees, "Okay I ain't gotta work," Jordan runs through the yard, opens the door, Vicky's sitting on the floor working on the puzzle at the coffee table asks, "Why are you in a hurry?"

Jordan goes to his old room, "I lost track of time, I got to be at work in 20 minutes," he is in his closet looking for his uniform.

Vicky stands up asks, "So you gonna need a ride to work?"

Jordan comes out of his room, goes to the bathroom yells, "Relax mom, Reign is gonna give me a ride."

"Oh okay, how come she didn't come in?"

Jordan from the bathroom explains, "I told her to wait in the car. I didn't want to get caught up in a long conversation, I can't be late to work too many more times."

"Well hopefully, I'll get a chance to meet her soon. So how are things with your dad?"

Jordan walks into the living room putting his shirt on. "It's cool, I don't see him too much he works long hours at the car lot, and the sofa bed is not too uncomfortable."

"So, what are you eating?"

Jordan walks to the door, "Between microwave dinners and work I'm good."   He opens the door. "Got to go."

Vicky follows behind Jordan and he turns around and looks at her tells him in a soft tone. "Just because I sent you to your father does not mean I abandoned you. Call me if you need anything." She hugs him.

Jordan hugs her back. "Thanks," he runs out across the yard. Vicky still at the door, waves at Reign. She waves back. Jordan jumps in the car.

Reign starts the car while driving she looks at Jordan, "I didn't know you lived on this street I want to show you something real quick." She drives down the block and on the same side as Jordan's house is a house that has a **SOLD** sign in the front yard. The house is a ranch-style single-story white brick house with a long driveway on a slight hill leading to the garage with a single tree in the middle of the front yard.

Jordan looks at Reign asks, "Why are we parked here? I got to get to work."

Reign looks back at Jordan, with some excitement in her voice, "We are moving soon and this is our new house."

Jordan surprised, "You playing with me?"

Reign driving away chuckles, "No I'm not."

Jordan excitedly asks, "When?"

Reign responds, "I think sometime next week, my dad is out of town because of his job, so it won't be until he comes home."

Jordan still excited exclaims, "Dope."

Tristan and Dejuan are sitting in the car in front of Reign's house, finishing up a joint.

Tristan looks at his dashboard clock, "Look bro we've been sitting here for almost two hours." He starts the car. "I'm out."

"Hold up I'm trying her one last time." He calls Reign it goes straight to voice mail, he hangs up the phone, angrily shouts, "You go ahead bro I ain't going nowhere." He opens the door and gets out of the car.

"So, what you just gonna wait out in her front yard?"

Dejuan gets out of the car slams the door snarls, "Don't worry about it."

Tristan looks at Dejuan standing outside the car. "Bro, look at yourself she got you all salty." He pulls into her driveway turns around, and starts driving away.

Dejuan runs after him yelling and waving his arms. "Yo T hold up, hold up, I need my headphones." Tristan hears this and looks at the rearview mirror, he stops the car. Dejuan runs to the passenger side opens the door, "I need my headphones." Tristan grabs them from the center console, he reaches over and hands them to Dejuan. He gets in, "You know what you right bro, let's go."

Tristan takes off again. "Welcome back to earth, she got you out here acting sus."

Dejuan moans, "I don't know bro, she just drives me crazy." A red Camaro passes by them Dejuan excited, "Oh shit that's Reign turn around."

Tristan, "What fool? I ain't turning around I got somewhere to be. It's obvious she doesn't want to see you."

Dejuan yells, "I don't give a shit about that! Turn around! I need to talk to her."

Tristan pulls into a driveway and turns around, shakes his head says, "Damn fool she got you acting extra."

Reign pulls up in the driveway, she and Zoey get out of the car, and walk to the front door. Tristan parks right in front of the house. Dejuan gets out of the car and runs across the yard he yells, "Reign! Reign!"

Reign is so shocked by Dejuan's sudden appearance she drops her house keys. "What are you doing here?" Zoey picks them up and gives them back to her and then holds her hand.

Dejuan says, "I've been trying to call you all day, where you been?"

Reign snaps, "Don't worry about it, it's none of your business, I told you we are not going out anymore, don't' call, don't text, just leave me alone."

Dejuan persists, "You been gone all day, so, where were you?"

"How do you know I've been gone all day? Have you been here at my house?"

Dejuan ignores her comment, "You been with that fool from the Burger House?"

Zoey pulls on Reign's arm, "I really want to go in the house."

Reign tells Dejuan, "I'm going in the house so you need to leave."

Dejuan grabs her arm, "I told you I not letting you go, why won't you give me another chance?"

Reign snatches her arm away, loudly exclaims, "Why can't you understand I don't want to be with you anymore? Now go!"

Zoey pulls on Reign's hand pulling her down a little, "I'm scared can we please go in the house."

Reign more calmly asks, "Please DJ can you just leave?"

"Okay, but I'll be seeing you around." He turns and walks across the front yard.

Reign watches him until he gets in the car, then opens the front door.

Zoey after they are in the house asks, "Are you going to tell Jordan?"

Reign shrugs, "I don't know if I should he already got kicked out of his momma's house, he doesn't need any more problems. If I keep ignoring DJ he will figure it out."

Zoey says in a statement wise beyond her years, "Are you trying to convince me or yourself?"

CHAPTER SIXTEEN

It's getting dark and Vicky pulls up to Keith's apartment security gate. She looks at Jordan and asks, "You know the code?"

Jordan tells her, "161211"

She punches it in and the gate opens. She drives through the complex until she comes to his building. She sees Keith's blue BMW 440i is not in his normal parking spot.

"I see your dad is not here."

"Yeah, I don't see him too much. We just have different work schedules."

Vicky replies, "I'm not sure it was the best thing for me to send you over here, sounds like you are on your own."

Jordan shrugs shoulders. She continues, "I will talk to him. Well, let me get back. Gotta get up early for work."

Jordan opens the door. "Okay." He gets out and runs up the stairs.

Vicky drives out of the complex and at the gate she sees Keith's blue BMW as he is coming in the gate. He drives through, and stops, and lets down his window. She pulls up next to him.

"What's up, V?"

"Just dropping Jordan off. Are you spending any time with him?"

Keith chuckles a little ask, "What are you talking about?"

"I'm asking. It just seems like every time I see him you are not around."

"I had a life before he came here, and you just dropping him on me without warning, I'm not going to change my life for this."

"The reason I sent him over is so you and him can have an actual father-son relationship."

"Well, you do know it wasn't just going to happen overnight. He rubs his chin, "So what about you and me, and our relationship?"

Vicky shakes her head, mildly amused by Keith's audacity. "One relationship at a time Keith, I gotta go." She lets up her window and drives away.

Keith rolls up his window and drives to his apartment.

Keith opens the door, Jordan is in the recliner, on his phone.

Keith brings in some food. "What's up J hope you hungry."

Jordan hops up off the recliner, walks to the dining table, "Sure am. What you got?"

Keith says, "I just stopped by Chicken King grabbed an 8-piece dinner meal."

Jordan sits at the table. Keith grabs a plate and puts it in front of Jordan, Jordan grabs a thigh and leg. Keith sits down.

"I saw your mom. She asked me how we're doing, and now I'm asking you. How do you think we are doing?"

Jordan taking a deep breath and replies, "Well I think we're good."

"So, is that what you told your mom?"

Jordan replies, "Well yeah, that and we don't see each other too much because of work."

"Do you like living here?"

Jordan nods and says, "So far, you've been cool, you don't treat me like a baby and I don't have to babysit KJ or Ericka."

Keith laughs, "Thanks I know you're not a little boy anymore," he takes a bite of chicken before he gets up to asks, "Do you want some tea?"

"Sure."

Keith gets the tea out of the fridge, and Jordan gets up and grabs two glasses.

Keith pours the tea in Jordan's glass first and tells him, "I like having you here, when you were younger, I wasn't ready to be a dad, I was young and stupid trying to still hang out and do my thang. When your momma called and told me what you were doing, it sounds just like me at your age. I realized that it is my responsibility as your father to help you avoid some of the mistakes I made if you will let me."

Jordan grabs the glass drinks some tea and complains, "I just think mom still treats me like a little kid. Next year I'll be a senior."

Keith gets up from the table looks at Jordan, "That's just her maternal instincts, not wanting to let go, to her you are always going to be her little boy."

Jordan sighs, "Yeah I guess"

Keith walks to the sink. "I got plans to go out of town this weekend you are going to have to stay with your mother."

Jordan is surprised, "What? Why?"

Keith looks at Jordan, "Look your mother would flip her wig if she knew you were staying here by yourself."

"I got to work this weekend and I'm closing so all I'm going to be doing is work and sleep."

Keith takes a deep breath and asks, "So how are you gonna get back and forth to work?"

"Both Nick and Reign have a car, I'll catch a ride with one of them."

Keith drops his plate in the sink. "Let me think about it. I will get back to you. Right now, I got a meeting with a friend."

He walks down the hall into his room and shuts the door.

Jordan grabs another piece of chicken. He picks up his phone and continues playing his online chess game.

After 30 minutes Keith comes out of his room freshly showered and walks to the living room asks, "So what do you think?" He's trimmed down his beard, put a small diamond stud in his left ear, he's wearing a black paisley long-sleeved tribal print shirt, black cuffed slacks, and some black leather oxford shoes.

Jordan sits up in the recliner and replies, "Nice! So, this is not a business meeting?"

"Definitely not, I'm trying something new I met this honey on a dating app."

"So, what's her name?"

"Lyric, I got to get going I'm supposed to meet her at Jack's in twenty minutes."

Keith puts on his glasses and opens the door and turns around, "No company," he states. "See you in the morning."

Jordan smiles back. "Aight pops."

Keith shuts the door.

Jordan lays back down on the recliner, and opens his phone he's got a text message from Spenser, *Check out your Instagram.*

Jordan goes to it the last post it reads, *you better stay away from Reign.*

CHAPTER SEVENTEEN

Jordan sits up in the recliner, mutters quietly, "What the fuck?" He calls Reign her phone rings she answers after 5 rings.

Jordan stands up and yells, *"Yo did you see what that fool posted on my gram."*

Reign is at home in her living room, *"What? What are you talking about?"* She gets up and walks to her bedroom and shuts the door.

Jordan's pacing back and forth in the living room at his father's apartment, *"That nigga's posting I better stay away from you."*

Reign sits on her bed. *"Oh shit, really?"*

"Yeah, you need to come by and get me so I can set this fool straight."

Reign in a quiet calm voice, *"Chill J, I just got home from work I 'm tired, I not coming to get you. I will talk with DJ to make sure he understands we are over."*

"Aight if you say so, I ain't no punk I'm not going to have this fool threatening me without me doing something."

"I know you ain't no punk, I told you I was going to talk to him let me handle it." She changes the subject, *"You know we haven't talked all day so what's been up?"*

Jordan sits back on the couch. *"Well work was cool, I got home me and my dad talked, he said he's probably going out of town this weekend so I'm need a ride to work if that's cool."*

"We'll see. So, he is going to let you stay there by yourself while he's gone?"

"I think he will."

"So, when you going to find out?"

"Later this week. Can you come by and see me tomorrow at work?"

Reign replies, *"I'm not sure, my mom wants to start packing stuff up, hit me up before you go on break, and we will see."*

Jordan's phone buzzes. He looks at it and it's a text from Spenser: *Did you see it?*

Jordan reassures her, *"Okay, I can do that. Gotta go. See you tomorrow."*

Reign smiles, *"See you tomorrow, goodnight."* She hangs up.

Jordan immediately calls Spenser, who answers after the first ring.

"Don't say nothing fool, I saw it."

Spenser laughs, *"Just checking bro, what's up with him?"*

Jordan snaps, *"I don't know I haven't seen that fool, since him and Reign came to eat, I guess since Reign told him they were done he's a little salty."*

Spenser warns, *"I don't know that fool but if I was you I definitely would be watching my back."*

Jordan promises, *"I'm good. Reign is going to talk with him to set him right."*

Spenser assures him, *"Aight if anything happens I got your back."*

Jordan calms down and changes the subject. *"Cool, so what's been up?"*

Spenser replies, *"Not much, just chillin trying to spend some time with Chloe."*

Jordan laughs, *"That's what's up. So, you and her are a thing now?"*

Spenser responds, *"Working on it, what's up with you?"*

Jordan sighs, *"Well you know my mom kicked me out, I'm at my dad's place, me, and Reign are working on our thing too."*

Spenser loudly exclaims, *"Damm, your mom kicked you out? Why?"*

Jordan *explains, "That day we smoked in the car, and KJ had a dentist appointment. She went off, and kicked me out to live with my dad."*

Spenser asks, *"So how is that working?"*

Jordan replies, *"You know cool so far. We don't see each other, with the hours he works, he's talking about going out of town this weekend."*

Spenser excitedly suggests, "Yo bro you outa have a kickback."

Jordan dismissively answers, "Bro I'm working the whole weekend, and if he does go I might have to stay with my mom while he is out of town."

Spenser says, "Damn that would be messed up."

Jordan retorts, "I'm not worried about it, I just want to get with Reign."

Spenser teases, "Yeah I wouldn't either not with her ex about to kick your ass."

Jordan, "Whatever fool, later."

Reign texts Dejuan: *"What's up with the post on Jordan's Instagram,"* she lays down on her bed and, places the phone on her pillow.

She is dozing off when her phone pings, it's Dejuan's blocked number. She calls him back.

DJ coolly asks," *What's up boo?*

Reign sits up and angrily responds, "*What's your deal with threatening Jordan?*"

"It wasn't a threat it was a warning."

"Why can't you understand that we're through?"

"Why won't you just give me another chance?"

Reign sighs," *I'm tired of playing this game, I'm sorry I'm not trying to hurt you I just think this is the best thing if we both go our separate ways.*"

DJ pleads, *"I'm not ready to let you go, whatever problems we had we can talk about it and work it out."*

Reign raises her voice, *"We are doing it right now."* She talks louder, *"Just let me go we have only been together for 5 months it wasn't that serious we were just having fun."*

His voice raises, *"To you maybe, I love you. You were the best thing that ever happened to me."*

Reign in a serious tone, *"Look here it is. We are done move on. I'm seeing Jordan now."*

DJ threatens, *"Look I warned that nigga not to see you again, next time I might not be so nice."*

Reign *demands, "Don't do something stupid that you will regret."*

"The only one who is gonna regret anything is Jordan if you keep seeing him." He angrily hangs up. She drops the phone on the bed as DJ's threat echo's in her head.

CHAPTER EIGHTEEN

Reign is in her room. There are moving boxes on her bed, the dresser drawers are open. She's pulling clothes out folding them and placing them in the boxes.

Her mom Dawn peeks her head in. "So, how's the packing coming?"

Reign throws a pair of socks into a box "Okay I guess."

Dawn walks into the room and sits on the bed, "Something wrong?"

Reign sits down on the bed across from her, "Well me and DJ broke up."

"I'm sorry honey, are you, all right?"

"I'm good, I broke it off with DJ, and he's the one tripping."

"What he does?"

"Well, last night he threatened a friend on Instagram."

"A friend? Who is this friend? Is this somebody I know? How did he threaten him?"

Reign laughs, "Slow down with all the questions, let me see, well the friend's name is Jordan, and no you don't know him. We are taking it slow just getting to know each other. DJ posted something on Instagram about him."

"So, has DJ ever hurt you? Is that why you're breaking up with him?"

"No, he hasn't hurt me. He has just gotten so jealous lately, crowding my space."

Dawn places her hand on Reign's and looks directly at her. "Now you would tell us if he hurt, wouldn't you?"

Reign assures her, "Yeah mom sure."

"I don't want you to be afraid to tell us anything."

Reign stands up, "I know. So, when are we moving?"

"Hopefully when your dad gets back in town next week, we can finish the paperwork. If I had to guess it's at least going to be another 2 weeks."

Reign asks, "Well practice starts this week, is it okay if I go?"

"Sure, just make sure you're all packed up."

Reign phone buzzes on the bed, Dawn grabs it and reads the text aloud, *"I'm on break for 20 minutes."*

She reaches down and grabs the phone from her, "Give me that."

"So, who is that from?"

Reign explains, "It's Jordan the friend I was just talking about, I told him I would try to meet him when he has a break."

"Sounds like he is becoming more than just a friend."

"I told you we were taking it slow," she states as she grabs her car key fob.

"So, am I going to get to meet him?"

Reign stands at the bedroom door, "Of course the house we are moving to is on his street."

Dawn stands up smiling replies, "That's a pretty freaky coincidence."

Reign smiles back, "Yeah I know maybe the universe is putting us together."

Dejuan knocks on Tristan's apartment door. Tristan opens it, "You again fool. What's up?"

"Yo I'm hungry give me a ride to Burger House."

Tristan responds, "What? You still owe for that weed we smoked last week."

"Look run me to Burger House and I got you."

"Aight, let's go," Tristan says, as they walk out the door. "Yo I hope you don't be trippin like the last time."

"I'm good, just trying to get something to eat."

Tristan unlocks the doors. "Cool you were buggin bro. She got you strung out. She must have really put it on you."

Dejuan gets into the car, "Keeping it 100 she does know how to work it. It just fucks with my head thinking that she might be doing some other nigga."

Tristan backs out of the space and drives down the street. "So, you over her now?"

Dejuan looks out the car window. "I don't need to get over her, I need to get with her."

Tristan chuckles, "So I take that as a no."

Jordan sits in the empty dining area, with his phone out playing the same chess game.

Reign walks through the door and yells, "What's up?"

Jordan looks up and waves, "What's up boo, you want something to drink?"

Reign sits down across the table, "Sure I'll take a lemonade."

Jordan goes to the counter, grabs a large cup, and gets the lemonade. When he comes back to the table he hands it to Reign and asks, "So did you talk with your boy?"

Reign shakes her head up and down, "Yeah."

Jordan prompts, "Ok sooo what's up?"

Reign sips on the lemonade. "Well the talk didn't go so well, he still thinks me and him have a chance."

"You told him it was over right?"

"Yes, he just isn't getting it."

Jordan suggests, "Maybe I need to talk to him straight up."

Reign hesitates. "I don't know if that's a good idea, he is a fool."

Jordan blows up, "Yeah I know he is a fool, but I need to let him know I ain't no punk. I can't have this nigga threatening me and nothing happening."

Reign drinks some more lemonade. "Chill no one thinks you're a punk, all he's doing is talking, don't overreact, and do something crazy."

Jordan breathes deeply and shakes his head. "Whatever, I just don't trust that fool."

Reign grabs his hand, "Relax I'm with you not him. Let's see where this goes, I'm tired of talking about DJ. Hey, I got practice coming up Saturday."

"Cool, cool I was talking with Spenser, he suggested if my father goes out of town that I should have a kickback. What do you think?"

Reign shrugs. "Yeah, I guess, what day?"

"Saturday. I'm supposed to work, will see. What's your schedule like?"

"Well I got practice that morning, and I go into the store and don't get off until six. Who's coming?"

"I don't know, my boys Nick and Spenser and whoever they bring, it's going to be small just chilling watching Netflix." He looks at his phone. "Got to get back to work."

He gets up then she stands up, they are holding hands, looking at each other she smiles at him quietly says, "Well what you gonna do?"

He smiles back at her and goes in for the kiss, they passionately tongue wrestle for five, six seconds he lets go of her hands and hugs her waist, as she puts her hands on his shoulders and gently pushes him away, "I gotta go finish packing and you need to go to work."

Jordan smiles, "You about to get something started."

Dejuan walks in with Tristan behind him, just in time to sees Jordan and Reign kissing. He immediately turns around and walks out.

Tristan follows behind, "Yo what's up?"

Dejuan walks to the car goes to the passenger door and hits the top of the car, "Let's go I'ma come back later and set this fool straight."

CHAPTER NINETEEN

Keith walks into the living room carrying a black leather overnight bag. Jordan's lying on his stomach asleep on the couch. Keith shakes him on his shoulder.

Jordan turns over, looks at Keith groggily. "What's up?"

"I'm going to Houston for the weekend, I'm leaving right after work."

Jordan sits up, "Cool, so I gotta go stay with mom till you get back?"

Keith moves Jordan aside and sits down on the couch beside him. "Well I thought about it, and I believe this is a chance to show what type of man you are."

"Okay and?"

"I mean I'm giving you a chance to either show that you are becoming a mature adult I can trust or…

Jordan excitedly asks, "So that means I can stay here for the weekend?"

Keith takes a really deep breath before replying, "I learned a saying 'A man needs a chance to do wrong to show that he will do right.' Look you have to promise me that you're not going to do anything stupid while I'm gone."

"All I'm doing is working and sleeping this weekend."

Keith inquires, "So you going to be able to get to work?"

"Yeah between Reign and Nick I should be good."

Keith stands up and picks up his bag. "I'm leaving right after work, so I won't see you again until Monday."

Jordan asks, "So who are you going out of town with? Is it the same one you took out earlier this week?"

Keith laughs, "Naw that was just Lyric, I was just getting to know her, this is Madison an old friend from back in the day."

Jordan declares, "Man you an OG playa."

Keith walks to the door. "I'll text you this weekend to check on you." He opens the front door says, "Later."

"Cool." Jordan lies back down and starts thinking about how he's going to spend the weekend before he drifts off back to sleep.

Two hours later Jordan's awake and sitting up on the couch, checking out his phone. He texts Nick and Spenser in a group text: *Check it out fools my pops is going out of town for the weekend.*

He then texts Reign: *My pops is headed out of town for the weekend. Can I get a ride to work?* He drops his phone on the couch and lays back down, he turns the TV on and drifts off to sleep.

After 20 minutes his phone dings its Reign, *What time do you have to be at work?*

Jordan: 6.

Reign texts: *I don't get off till 6.*

Jordan: *Ok I can see if Nick can give me a ride.*

Nick texts Jordan: *Cool so the kickback is on!*

Jordan texts back: *What, fool, I told you I got to work tonight.*

Nick: *So, call in it's the perfect setup, Reign's off, I can bring by Za'dora, Spenser can bring Chloe, it just works bro.*

Jordan drops his phone on the couch and sits back. He thinks, *Should I do it? Reign is off, we can finally get some alone time together, I can't blow this chance. I'll just call in it's not like it's my first time.*

Jordan sits back up and group texts Nick and Spenser: *Let me check to see if Reign is down.*

Jordan to Reign: *Can you come through for the kickback?*

Reign texts back: *I thought you had to work?"*

Jordan: *I'm call in so we good.*

Reign: *Who else is going to be there?*

Just my bros Nick and Spenser and whoever they bring it's going to be small.

Reign: *I should be able to make it, just hope I'm not too tired, just text me the address.*

Jordan texts back: *Cool, I will meet you at the front security gate, we can run to the store to get some munchies.*

Reign: *OK cu then.*

Jordan group's text Nick and Spenser: *It's on at 8.*

Spenser texts back: *Cool I got the smoke covered, just make sure we have something to drink.*

Jordan takes a deep breath to think about what to say when he calls in. He calls, Mark his shift manager answers the company phone.

Mark: *What's up Jordan?*

Jordan: *I'm not going to be in today, my mother got called into work so I have to watch my little sister and brother.*

Mark: *This is your third time calling in this month, I don't know how many more chances you are going to get.*

Jordan: *I know, my mom just told me a few minutes ago. I got to go see you later.*

Mark. *Later.*

At 7:30 pm. Jordan is outside the security gate. When Reign pulls up he jumps in the car. Reign pulls up to the gate, as Jordan is putting on his seat belt.

"The code is 169211, hope you can remember that in case you need it later."

Reign laughs and puts in the code, "Sure yeah, will see."

Reign goes through the gate and turns around, "So where are we going?"

"There is a grocery store down the street, just going to get a few bags of chips and some juice."

Reign looks at him and asks in a serious tone, "Should you be doing this?"

"It will be cool, it's not like we are having a full-blown party, just my bro's Nick and Spenser and their baes."

"So, does your dad know you're doing it?"

"Well not exactly. He is out of town doing his thing."

Reign stops at a traffic light.

"I'm not sure I like where this is going."

Jordan laughs, "Don't stress. We are just going to hang out."

Nick and Spenser are parked at the Hills Point Projects, basketball courts.

Nick asks, "So where your boy at?"

"Look fool, I don't know he texted me that he would meet us at 7:30."

Nick looks at the car clock, "It's 7:37."

Spenser looks at him, "Really bro? You didn't believe exactly 7:30? Come on now, you know about cpt."

Nick looks at Spenser, "Whatever bro, text him to see where he's at."

Spenser answers, "Aight" and grabs his phone, just as he is about to text, Tristan pulls up on Spenser's side of the car. Tristan lets down the window yells, "What's up Spens?"

Spenser lets down his window and looks over at Tristan and asks, "What up T? What you got?"

Tristan, "Whatever you need."

Spenser looks over at Nick, "So what you think we should get?"

"How much money you got?"

Spenser looks at him throws his hands up. "Really bro, this again?"

Nick checks the middle storage compartment, grabs a single 10-dollar bill, "Here."

He hands it to Spenser, he grabs a 20 out of his pocket looks at Nick, "Yo I'm go to his car I don't want him skimping on us." He opens the door, and shuffles around the front of the car, and jumps in Tristan's car.

Tristan looks at him, "So how much you got?"

Spenser replies, "I got 30, that's good for an eighth?"

Tristan leans back and grabs his gym bag from the back seat, unzips it, and grabs a scale and a small medicine bottle with weed in it. He puts the scale on the car dashboard puts a couple of buds on the scale it reads 3.5 grams. He grabs a plastic sandwich bag and puts the buds in it. Spenser gives him the money and Tristan throws the money in the gym bag.

Spenser grabs the weed, opens the door, "Cool, cool see you around."

Tristan asks, "So what's up?"

Spenser gets out of the car, "My boy is having a little kickback, later tonight."

Tristan asks as Spenser gets back in Nick's car, "Anybody I know?"

"Just my boy Jordan, later bro," Nick backs out and drives off.

CHAPTER TWENTY

As Nick drives away he asks Spenser, "You know how to get to Jordan's place?"

"No, I never been over there. What about the girls?"

Nick comes to a stoplight. "Chloe is picking up Za'dora. Maybe we can meet somewhere and they can follow us."

"Look you call Chloe and I will call Jordan to get directions."

"Bet."

Jordan's in the living room, vacuuming the carpet, Reign's in the kitchen loading up the dishwasher.

Jordan's phone buzzes on the kitchen table, Reign hearing it yells, "Jordan, Jordan," he doesn't hear her over the vacuum cleaner, she grabs the phone and takes it to him.

Jordan turns off the vacuum and answers the phone, "Yo what's up?"

Nick asks, "Yo where you live? Neither me nor Spenser been there since you got kicked out."

"I'll text it to you. Who's coming with you?"

"Spencer is calling Chloe and her girl Za'Dora we going to meet them, then they're going to follow us to your place."

"Cool just text me when you're at the gate so I can let you in."

"Aight see you in a few."

Meanwhile, Spenser's talking with Chloe, "What's up girl? You still coming through?"

Chloe gets into her car, "Yeah, I was just headed to pick up Za'dora, What's up?"

Spenser, "Me and Nick were thinking we could meet you somewhere and you follow us."

Chloe starts her car and replies, "Sounds like a plan, it's gonna take me about 20 minutes to get Za'dora, that's if she's ready."

Spencer tells her, "Alright just hit me back when you get here, cu tonight."

Jordan hangs up the phone, puts it on the coffee table, and turns to Reign, "That was Nick just trying to get directions."

Reign asks, "So I guess everything is on?"

"Yeah, you don't sound happy, everything cool?'

Reign sits down on the couch. "I don't know I just feel funny, about you not telling your father."

Jordan sits down beside her, "Chill, you know everybody who's coming, it's just going to be a small thing. My pops ain't coming back till Monday, everything will be back to normal by then."

Jordan grabs his phone off the coffee table, "I gotta text Nick the address."

Jordan and Reign are at the front gate waiting for Nick and Spenser, Nick's gray Accord pulls into the complex, and right behind it is an older black Hyundai Sonata.

Nick lets down his window, yells "What up bro?"

Jordan steps to the keypad punches in the code and jumps in the back seat," It's about time y'all showed up."

Reign goes to the other car, Chloe lets down her window, "Hop in girl." Reign jumps in the backseat.

Chloe follows behind Nick. She introduces them, "Reign this is Za'dora." Za'dora is a coca brown sister with long black curly hair tied with an orange scrunch which hangs over her left shoulder she has on a matching orange shirt and blue jeans and a clear backpack with orange flowers on it. She reaches back and shakes her hand, Za'dora, "Nice to meet you." Reign replies, "Same here."

Za'dora asks Chloe, "So how do y'all know each other?"

Chloe explains, "We play summer ball on the same team. So, you going to be at practice tomorrow?"

Reign replies, "Yeah, thanks for holding my spot."

Chloe pulls into the parking spot, "Girl you know you know I'm holding a spot for 'Purple Reign.'"

Reign laughs, the boys have already parked their car and are getting out.

Za'dora asks, "So which one I'm supposed to be hanging with?"

Reign questions, "Oh you don't know them?"

Chloe points at Nick, "It's him."

Za'dora turns around explains to Reign, "We talked a couple of times on the phone and a couple of Instagram posts, this our first in-person meet." She gets out of the car checks him out says, "He could be my bae."

Reign gets out of the car and runs up to Jordan, and grabs his hand.

Chloe and Za'dora walk up to Spenser and Nick, Chloe walks up to Spenser and he hugs her, "What's up girl?"

Chloe answers, "What's Up" she then turns and looks at Za'dora, "This is Nick," he walks up to her does the, "What's up" head nod, Za'dora responds accordingly.

Jordan still holding Reign's hand says loudly, "Cool now that everybody knows each other let's go upstairs."

Spenser grabs Chloe's hand, "Just waiting on you bro."

They all go upstairs, Jordan opens the apartment door. "Okay everybody come in and take a seat,

Spenser goes straight to the recliner, Nick, Chloe, and Za'dora head to the couch.

Jordan walks into the kitchen, "I'm getting a couple of chairs from the kitchen," he looks at Reign asks, "Can you bring the snacks out?"

"Sure."

Jordan grabs two chairs and from the kitchen takes them to the living room, Reign follows behind him with two large white bowls one has potato chips the other has Doritos. She set them on the coffee table and goes back and gets some paper plates and a roll of paper towels.

Jordan sits down on one of the kitchen chairs and Reign sits in the other chair beside him.

Jordan offers, "Alright there are some drinks in the fridge and some cupcakes in the kitchen."

Spenser asks, "So what's the plan?"

Jordan answers, "I thought you knew we'd listen to some music, watch some Netflix, play Uno, and see what happens."

Chloe laughing asks, "Uno? Are you talking about the card game? I haven't played that in years."

Jordan a little offended, "What? You don't like Uno?"

Chloe still laughing. "Naw it's cool," reaches over and grabs a handful of chips out of the bowl.

Nick inquires, "So what's on Netflix?"

Jordan gets up and grabs the remote from the side pouch in the recliner that Spenser is sitting in, turns on the television. "I've been watching that show Cobra Kai, my dad turned me on to it, he said he liked that old movie Karate Kid."

Nick sits up on the couch and grabs some Doritos, "I heard of it but never watched it."

Za'dora chimes in, "Yeah I watched the first season, haven't seen the second season yet."

Jordan turns it on, Spenser gets up, "Yo J can I put on some music?"

Jordan gets up, "Yeah let me get the speaker out of my pop's room."

Za'dora asks, "Can you turn on the subtitles, if I can't hear it at least I can read it."

Spenser chuckles, "I don't know anybody who uses subtitles."

Jordan gets up and walks to his father's room.

Reign gets up and goes to the kitchen she grabs the package of 6 chocolate cupcakes and places them on the coffee table.

Za'dora asks Reign, "So you play ball with Chloe?"

"Yeah, we play with the Suns. You play?"

Za'dora replies, "I did in middle school, now I play softball and run track."

Nick sits up when he hears this asks, "So what do you run in track?"

Za'dora turns towards Nick and tells him, "I run the 100 and 200 and play center field in softball."

Nick nods his head approvingly replies, "I run track too, the 800m and long jump" he gets up and sits next to Za'dora forcing Chloe to scoot over.

Spenser sits up in the recliner asks, "So how come your name is Za'dora?"

"I was named after my after my grandma, my friends call me Dora."

"You mean like from like the old Nick TV show?" Spenser asks.

"Yeah sure."

Jordan comes back into the living room carrying a small box speaker, with a round crystal ball on top of it. He turns on Pandora radio.

Dance' by Megan The Stallion is playing Chloe gets up and starts twerking.

Spenser excited by this yell, "Now that's what I'm talking about" he gets up and starts grinding on her as she leans back into it enjoying the ride.

Jordan gets up and goes to the kitchen grabs a bottle of Malibu coconut rum and a fifth bottle of Jim Beam Tennessee Whiskey, he yells over the music, "We bout to get turnt up," moves the cupcakes to the side, and places the bottles on the coffee table.

"I didn't know there was gonna be drinking, I don't drink," Za'Dora says nervously.

Nick puts his arm around her says. "Yo it's good nobody is making you do anything."

Jordan grabs 2 cups and starts making a drink with the coconut rum and coke. Reign puts her hand out refusing the drink, and says, "You don't remember I don't drink either."

Spenser still dancing with Chloe grabs the drink.

Reign grabs her phone out and starts taping Chloe and Spenser dancing, she then turns her phone around to do the selfie she says, "We at my new boyfriend Jordan's kickback" he then squeezes in the frame kisses her on her left cheek, throws up the peace sign and yells "What up!" Reign laughs and kisses him on the cheek, she then turns the phone back around and records Chloe and Spenser still grinding one another.

Reign records a little more, she stands up, "I need to use the bathroom. Where is it?"

Jordan turns around and points down the hall. "My dad's room is on the right the bathroom is across the hall."

Dora's phone buzzes, she pulls it out of her backpack.

Nick curiously leans over and tries to look at her phone asks, "So who is it?"

Dora smirks at him, "And how does that concern you?"

Nick sits back, "I'm just asking."

"It's my momma just checking up on me." She texts: *I'm just hanging with my girl Chloe should be home in a few hours,* she puts the phone back in her backpack.

"Now what were you saying?"

Nick responds, "Just asking what else you like to do?"

Spenser stops dancing and pulls the bag of weed out of his front pocket, "J you got any paper?"

Jordan stands up answers, "Yeah, my pops got some in his room."

Dora sees the weed and loudly protest, "Yo I ain't tryin to be around no weed, if y'all about to smoke I need to be out."

Nick asks, "What's the big deal?"

Dora stands up in a panicky state she repeats herself louder, "I am not going to stay if y'all smoking weed,"

Spenser stops dancing retorts, "Bye then."

Nick stands up yells at Spenser, "Yo bro shut the fuck up."

Spenser meekly answers back, "Whatever fool, I'm just tryin to have a good time."

Chloe stops dancing asks Dora, "Why you trippin so hard over weed?"

Dora and Nick sit back down. Jordan turns the music down, She answers, "My older brother used to smoke weed, he uses to get high every morning before he went to work as a roofer, about a year ago he had an accident where a metal shingle crowbar falls on him and crushed his skull. "

Chloe shocked cries, "OMG, did it kill him?"

Dora takes a deep breath sadly replies, "No but mentally he is not all there, he has really bad headaches all the time, and can't remember stuff, he's on worker's disability."

Chloe responds, "I had no idea. So, is he going to be like that for the rest of his life?"

Dora replies, "I don't like to talk about it, the Dr's don't really know how long it's going to last."

Spenser sitting back down in the recliner says quietly, "Great way to kill the vibe."

Reign comes back into the living room she sits down by Jordan, "What's going on I heard some yelling."

Jordan asks, "What were you doing?"

Reign looks at him, "I was posting the video on insta-gram."

Dora stands up, "I think I should go, I didn't mean to bring everybody down."

Reign asks, "What happened?"

Dora explains, "Everybody's having a good time, I don't want to ruin that." She looks at Chloe, "Can we leave?"

Spenser looks at Chloe, "Damn we were just starting to have a good time."

Chloe tells Spenser, "That's my girl I'm not going to leave her hanging."

Reign exasperated says, "I still don't know what happened."

Jordan looks at her, "I will tell you later."

Nick gives Dora his phone, "Here put your number in, Dora puts her number in and gives it back, Nick stands up takes a deep breath says to her, "I hate that you feel like you need to go but I don't want you to feel uncomfortable, maybe we can hookup just me and you, soon."

Dora shakes her head in agreement, "You got my number use it," she gives him a quick hug.

Spenser still sitting down pouts, "Damn she ruined the whole night."

Chloe kneels beside him and whispers, "Relax bro we still good, we got other days, besides I got practice in the morning," she reaches her hand between his crotch, squeezes him, and kisses him on the cheek she stands up says, "Dora, if you ready, let's go."

Spenser whines, "Girl that ain't even funny."

They walk to the door, Reign stands up and walks over to the door with them.

Chloe says to Reign, "Alright girl, you coming to practice."

"Of course, I'm getting ready to leave in a few minutes."

Chloe opens the door turns and hugs Reign and tells her, "Be good see you tomorrow."

Reign tells Dora, "It was nice meeting you. Hope to see you again."

Dora replies, "Nice meeting you too. Bye."

Dejuan's at home lying down on his bed when his phone dings. He grabs it off the nightstand and sees it's a post from Reign on her Instagram. He opens it up he sees it's the video from Jordan's kickback, he stares at it and squeezes his phone, getting angrier and angrier with all the laughing and dancing. When the video is over he throws his phone. It hits the wall across the room, he lays back down and swears to himself, *"I'm ending this tomorrow."*

CHAPTER TWENTY-ONE

Reign walks back to the couch and looks at Jordan and asks, "So what happened, with Za'Dora?"

Spenser answers instead, "Well we were all feeling the groove and having fun. When Nick was about to fire one up, she freaks out and starts talking about her brother getting knocked in the head with a crowbar at his job because he smoked weed."

"So that's why she got loud?" Reign asks.

Jordan replies, "I don't know what happened. One second she was chillin, and the next she was all depressed and sad."

Spenser slouches in the chair. "All I know is that me and Chloe were feelin each other."

Nick spouts out, "Bro, you weren't doing nothing,"

Spenser retorts, "Don't be hating Nick. Y'all want to fire up that joint?"

"Naw, I'm good dog. The mood is gone now," Jordan answers. "I'm just watchin' some Cobra Kai."

Nick and Spenser get up and walk to the door, and Jordan follows them.

Nick shakes Jordan's hand, "Aight bro will get with you."

Reign stands up. "I guess I should leave, too."

Spenser nods his head toward Reign and asks in a low voice, "So what's up with her?"

Jordan smiles and answers in a low voice, "Don't go their bro, she is leaving right behind you."

Spenser replies, "Okay, bro, yeah we know."

Jordan opens the door pushes and Spenser out onto the front porch "Get this fool out of here."

Nick walks out says, "Aight we'll get with you later."

Spenser outside the apartment pounds his right fist into his left palm and starts to laugh.

Jordan laughs too, "Whatever fool." He shuts the door.

Reign is at the front door face to face with Jordan. She tells him, "I'm about to go."

Jordan grabs her hand, looks her in the face, and pleads, "You sure you can't stay a few more minutes? It's still pretty early, we can catch a few shows of *Cobra Kai*."

Reign looks at him, pulls out her phone. It's 9:15. "Okay, but I'm leaving at ten I've still got practice in the morning."

Jordan still holding her hand, walks over to the couch.

They both sit down, he grabs the remote. "So, do you still want to watch Cobra Kai?"

"Sure, I can give it a chance."

He turns on Netflix. "This is where I left off."

"Cool", she responds, he puts his arm around her and she puts her head on his right shoulder.

She looks up at him and smiles. "This is nice."

He looks down at her says, "Yeah, I'm just glad you decided to stay."

She turns towards the TV asks, "What is this show about?"

"Well it's a long story, but it's a continuation of that Karate Kid movie from the '80s."

"I thought *The Karate Kid* was a Jaden Smith movie."

Jordan laughs, "That was a remake, and this show is from the original of course everybody is older and got kids now."

"So, have you seen the original?"

"Yeah, I watched it with my pops, then I started watching this."

"Alright, I guess I can give it a chance."

They are watching the show; Reign's head is resting on his right shoulder. He starts to run his hand down her French braid, she looks up at him with her big brown eyes, "Do you mind if I put my feet on the couch?"

"Of course not."

She takes off her slides puts her French manicured feet on the couch, of course, there painted royal purple. On the screen, the characters of Sam and Robby kiss. Jordan checks out Reign's ass in her black leggings, and thinks, "Damn she got a nice ass."

He puts his hand on her shoulder and runs it down her arm, to her hips, and gently grabs her ass.

She looks up at him, "I hope this show, ain't giving you no ideas."

"Actually, seeing how fine you are is giving me ideas," he answers, smiling at her.

She looks down and sees that he is getting an erection in his shorts, "I think I need to go before we start something."

"Are you sure you want to go?"

She stares at him, and sits up he stares back at her, and she whispers, "No."

His heart is beating 200 beats a minute, but he can't take his eyes off of her. He's stares at her apple-red full lips.

He whispers, "Damn you beautiful." He leans in and kisses her full tongue, rubbing her ass, she reaches her left hand underneath his shorts and starts massaging his penis.

She sits up suddenly, "I can't do this I got with DJ and he freaked out."

Jordan whispers quietly back, mind racing with anticipation heart still beating like a racehorse. "This is not my first time whatever we do or don't do is not going to send me over the edge and turn me into a psycho like your ex."

She has a small chuckle and smiles at him, "Do you have protection?"

"Yeah, of course."

Dejuan's laying down on his bed, Dezera his younger brother knocks on his door. DJ yells from the bed, "What you want?"

Dezera yelling back through the door, "There is somebody here to see you."

"So, who is it?"

"I don't know. He says he got something to tell you."

Dejuan jumps out of the bed rushes to the door and opens it and pushes Dezera out the way as he orders, "Move."

He walks into the living room and sees Tristan sitting on the couch. Surprised by this he asks, "What's up fool?"

Tristan stands up nervously, "I sent you a text, but you didn't hit me back so I came by. I think your girl is at a kickback with that fool she was kissing at the store?"

"And how do you know this?"

"A couple of his partners bought some smoke, said they were going to a kickback."

DJ answers, "Yeah, I checked out a video she posted earlier tonight, he asks, "Yo did they say where this fool stay at?"

"Nah bro, they just said they were getting it for a kickback."

"Yo I need you to come through tomorrow to run me by his job I'm setting this nigga straight."

"What are you going to do? What time?"

"I'm not sure, I 'll let you tomorrow."

Tristan walks to the front door, Dejuan opens it. "Thanks for the heads up."

Jordan gets up from the couch, Reign asks, "What time is it?"

Jordan grabbing his underwear grabs the TV remote. He hits the info button, it reads 10:22.

Panicky she jumps off the couch reaches for her panties. "Damn my mom's going to freak out."

Jordan puts on his shorts, "I'm sorry I just got caught up in the moment, part of this is your fault too you know."

Reign puts her bra on, "I just lost track of time. "She looks up at Jordan and assures him, "I enjoyed it."

Jordan agrees, "I had a good time myself, we going to have to get together again when we have more time."

Reign frantically gets dressed sits down puts on her leggings, "I just need to get home."

"So, what are you going to tell your mom?" Jordan asks.

She slips on her slides, grabs her phone, and checks her appearance on her phone. She smooths her hair and walks to the door. "I don't know. Maybe something about hanging with Chloe and Dora watching Netflix."

Jordan walking behind her, chuckles. "Well, part of that is true." He opens the door and follows behind her as she walks down the steps. She grabs her key fob clicks it. Jordan from behind grabs her left hand and pulls her in for a hug. He looks at her intently, "Thanks for coming through, I know it didn't go as planned but I'm glad you stayed."

Reign gives him a little peck on the lips smiling she says, "I'm glad too."

Jordan replies, "I don't want you to think that the only reason I asked you over is so we can smash. I really like you."

She looks at him smiles, "I like you too let's just see what happens. "I need to be going, I'm already late." She kisses him again, turns around opens the car door, she gets in. He asks, "Am I going to see you tomorrow?"

"Well, I got to practice in the morning, after that probably just helping my mother pack. How are you getting to work?"

"Hopefully you, I got to be there at 11. Is that cool?"

Reign shuts the door, starts her car, and rolls down her window. "Cool, I can pick you up after practice, be ready."

Jordan leans in and kisses her, "No worries."

CHAPTER TWENTY-TWO

Vicky and Ericka are in the living room sitting on the couch leaning over working on her puzzle when her phone rings.

She picks it up and reads, "Unknown number,"

She answers it a prerecorded women's voice speaks, "Hello, this is a collect call from Harris County, County Jail, from inmate Keith Skyy. Say yes if you will accept this call."

Vicky replies, "Yes."

Keith apologetically, "Hey baby, I hate to be calling you from here, but you the only one I could call."

Vicky angrily yells, 'Hey baby!' Why the hell are you calling me from jail? Where is Jordan?"

Keith hurriedly explains, "I don't have a lot of time to talk, I went out of town yesterday, with a friend, and coming back from the club, I got pulled over by the cops, and arrested."

Vicky probes, "So why did you get arrested? Where is Jordan?"

Keith replies, "I got pulled over for DUI and they arrested me because I got some warrants out." He pauses for a moment takes a deep breath and continues, "Jordan is still at my apartment."

Vicky loudly, "What!! Let me see if I got this straight. You went out of town for the weekend and left our 16-year-old son, unsupervised in your apartment, after all the shit he's been doing and you thought this was a good idea?"

Keith angrily explains, "I was trying to build a relationship with him, that I trust him. I just wanted to let you know, so you can check on him."

Vicky angrily responds, "'Check on him?' "He's coming home."

Keith in a calmer voice," Okay I understand. Could you help me get a lawyer?"

Vicky angrily responds, "Really? You only call when you need something, whoever you went out of town with she can help." She hangs up on him.

Vicky sits there quietly fuming staring into space trying to think about her next move.

Ericka stops working on the puzzle, and looks at Vicky asks, "What's wrong mom?"

She snaps out of it angrily answers, "My ex is a jackass. Every time I think there is some hope he does something to mess it up."

Standing up she yells, "KJ, let's go."

"Where we going?" KJ yells from his room.

"I need to talk to your brother now."

Vicky pulls into the crowded Burger House parking lot. "Stay here," she tells KJ sitting in the front and Ericka in the back.

"What's going on? You didn't talk the whole time." KJ says.

Vicky opens the car door about to get out when she stops, "Your father got arrested last night, and I need to tell Jordan."

KJ excitedly asks, "So Jordan is coming back home?"

"Yes, he is, tonight, after he gets off work."

KJ still excited, "Cool."

Vicky gets out of the car quietly less excited, "Yeah, cool."

Ericka yells from the backseat, "Get me a chocolate milkshake." KJ adds, "Me too."

Vicky looks back and shakes her head in agreement.

She walks into the restaurant and there is a long line waiting to order. There's a large lunch crowd today. She looks around and she sees Jordan with the drive-through headset on.

She walks around the crowd to the counter and calls "Jordan!" Then louder she calls again, "Jordan!"

He turns around surprised to see her, "What are you doing here?"

"We need to talk," she tells him.

"Right now?" he says with an incredulous look on his face, gesturing with his hands spinning his body around, to let her know it's not a good time.

She stares at him without an answer.

He takes the headset off, calls Brittany over. "Can you take over, for a minute? I got to go talk to my mom."

Brittany looks at Vicky, Vicky shoots her, a "don't asks any questions, just do it" look.

Brittany grabs the headset and puts it on she goes to the drive-through, Jordan opens the little door, "Let's go outside and talk," she tells Jordan.

"I don't have a lot of time," he tells her as he follows her outside.

She pulls him aside from the door, "Alright what's up?" Jordan asks.

"Your father just called me about 30 minutes ago, he's in jail."

"What?? What he do?"

"That's not important, I can't believe you didn't tell me he was going out of town."

"Why? If I did would you have let me stay over there?" Jordan asks.

"Of course not! Why would I? You're sixteen."

Jordan excitedly responds, "See that's exactly what I'm talking about."

Vicky excitedly gestures with her hands, "What are you talking about?"

"Dad treats me like a grown-up and you still treat me like a baby."

"After the way, you have been acting the last few weeks. How am I supposed to treat you?"

"All I know is dad doesn't baby me and we got along cool."

Vicky retorts, "Well that don't make no difference now. He's in jail, and you coming back home tonight."

Jordan turns and walks back into the restaurant, shakes his head "Whatever," he mumbles.

Vicky grabs his arm. He turns around looks at her. She directs him, "Call me after you get off, I'm picking you up."

CHAPTER TWENTY-THREE

Dejuan lay's in his bed with his headphones on listening to *"What It Feels Like"* by Nipsey Hustle.

When the phone chimes, he picks it up and gets pissed because the screen is cracked from when he threw it last night.

It's a text from Tristan: *Yo, you still need a ride to see this nigga.*

DJ: *Yeah, I need to set this fool straight, when can you come through?*

Tristan*: I'll be there in 20 be ready.*

Dejuan sits up grabs his jeans off the floor puts on his sliders, grabs his black backpack goes outside. He sits on the steps and puts back on his headphones.

Tristan pulls up to the front of Dejuan's apartment 24 minutes later. Dejuan jogs down the steps.

He jumps in the car, Tristan asks, "So what's the plan?"

"I'ma let him know that Reign is still my girl, and he needs to stay away from her."

Tristan inquires, "So what if he doesn't listen?"

Dejuan, in a serious tone, threatens, "Then I will make him listen."

Tristan asks, "How you plan on doing that?"

Dejuan irritated snaps, "You asks a lot of questions, don't worry about it I got it" he puts back on his headphones.

Tristan mumbles, "I don't even know why I run with you"

Dejuan takes off his headphones and glares at him, "You say something?"

Tristan continues to drive mumbles, "Naw fool."

Mark the manager comes up to Jordan at the drive-through window.

 Brittany's taking over the drive-through. It's slowed down so you can burn out early after you wipe down the tables and take out the trash."

Jordan hands the headset to Brittany. "Cool, maybe I can holla at Reign before I get out of here."

Brittany puts the headset on and asks, "So what was the deal with your mom today?"

Jordan explains, "She was trippin! My dad is in jail, and she bugging because I didn't tell her that he was going out of town for the weekend."

"So why is he in jail?"

"I don't know. She didn't tell me she just told me that I have to move back home."

Jordan walks to the dining room and mumbles, "Damn I know this is going to mess with my time with Reign."

He walks to the customer drink station reaches underneath the cabinet, and pulls out a rag and spray bottle, and starts spraying down the tables. Mark comes up behind Jordan grabs the rag, tells him, "I will wipe the tables down you go ahead and get the trash."

Jordan puts the spray bottle on the table, nonchalantly responds, "Cool" and walks to the back.

Tristan and DJ arrive at the Burger House, both get out of the car, DJ reaches in the back seat, grabs his backpack zips it open, and grabs a black 380 pistol. He shoves it in the left waistband of his jeans pulls down his blue t-shirt to cover it up.

They both walk to the door, Tristan glances at DJ, "You don't even know if he is here tonight, do you?"

"Nope", he answers as he walks through the door.

DJ walks cockily to the front counter. Brittany walks over from the drive-through to the front register.

DJ leans on the counter, looks at the menu, and tells her, "Give me a small sprite."

He stands back up, asks innocently, "Is Jordan working tonight?"

"Yeah," she answers looking around the dining room. "He must be out back dumping the trash."

DJ gets his soda, smiles at her, "See you around sweet thing."

She doesn't say anything she just smiles back.

He and Tristan walk out the side door to the back.

CHAPTER TWENTY-FOUR

Tristan follows DJ, they turn left and walk behind the restaurant.

Jordan has a large garbage bin and is pulling trash bags from it. His back is turned.

DJ sees this, and gives his drink to Tristan, then commands, "Hold this."

Jordan hears the noise without looking yells, "I'm glad somebody came to help me."

"Fool ain't nobody here to help you." DJ snarls at him.

Jordan turns around quickly looks at them its dark and he doesn't recognize them.

"Yo, what's up?"

DJ steps closer to Jordan, "I just came to tell you to stop messing around with Reign."

Jordan steps closer to DJ and recognizes him, sarcastically, "Ok you're Reign's ex, so you're here to tell me to stop messing with Reign?" His tone changes to a serious voice. "And what if don't?"

DJ suddenly pushes Jordan into the trash bin and he falls. DJ pulls out the gun, points it directly at Jordan's head. Tristan surprised by this drops the drink.

"Yo fool you didn't tell me that you were gonna smoke him, I ain't trying to be part of no murder."

DJ looks at him while still pointing the gun at Jordan. "Relax fool I got this." He walks closer to Jordan who is still on the ground he straddles him and points the pistol directly at his face, leans down, and puts the gun barrel on his forehead.

"I ain't going to smoke this fool, at least not yet. This is just a warning to let him know I'm serious. Next time he might not be so lucky."

Jordan's on the ground his face and body tense as he stares up at DJ. His heart is beating faster than the time he and Reign were together. Both his fist is clenched tightly, he doesn't say a word, he doesn't want to provoke DJ he knows he is in a precarious situation.

"Jordan you alright back here? We heard a commotion," Mark yells as he walks towards him.

Tristan hears this and urges, "Yo we need to go! Now!"

DJ straightens back up and puts the gun back in his waistband he spits on Jordan with it landing on his neck right under his chin. Yells at him, "Fuck you fool" he then takes off running behind Tristan.

Mark comes back there, sees Jordan on the ground, and helps him up, "You alright Jordan? You hurt?"

Jordan shrugs him off and uses the collar of his shirt to wipe the spit off his neck, he walks away from Mark, "I'm good I need to leave now."

"Are you going to finish cleaning the dining area?" Mark asks.

"I don't give a fuck about that," he says as he walks through the restaurant to the parking lot and sees that they are gone. He starts angrily pacing back and forth on the sidewalk. Shaking his head back and forth in anger. He pulls his phone out of his pocket and calls Nick.

Jordan to Nick excitedly, "Yo fool I need you to come gets me from work now."

"What's wrong?"

"That fool Dejuan came up here and pulled a piece on me."

"Damn, you for real?"

"Yo come get me I need to let this fool know what's up?"

"Bro, I was on my way to get Spenser to hang out with Dora and Chloe.

"What?? Later for that! You my boy or what?"

"Alright, 'bros before ho's give me 15 minutes."

"Cool hurry up."

Jordan still pacing on the sidewalk, Brittany comes outside. "Mark wanted me to come talk to you to see if everything is alright."

Jordan stops in front of Brittany and says, "That fool Dejuan threatened me and pulled a gun."

Brittany shakes her head. "So, what are you going to do?"

Jordan starts pacing again. "I don't know, my boy Nick is about to pick me up we gonna see if we can find this fool."

Brittany grabs his right arm as he passes by her, he looks at her as she pleads, "Don't do anything crazy"

Jordan, snatches his arm away and snaps, "Whatever," he looks at her and realizes that he is angry at the wrong person, "I'm sorry just go back in, I'll see you tomorrow"

Brittany turns to go. "Just remember what I said," she goes back inside.

Nick turns into the parking lot and pulls right up to the sidewalk. Jordan runs around the front and gets in the car.

Nick peels out and makes a u-turn as he asks Jordan, "So where we headed?"

Jordan responds, "That nigga was with Spenser's, boy Tristan who sold us the weed. Where he stay at?"

Nick replies, "I don't know, maybe Spens does."

Jordan pulls out his phone and calls, Spenser,

Jordan still excited talks fast, *"You know where your boy Tristan stays at?"*

Spenser caught off guard by Jordan's excitement answers, *"Yo bro slow down. What's going on?"*

"Your boy was with Dejuan, they came to the job and pulled a gun on me."

"No shit. Where you at now?"

"I'm with Nick we coming through to scoop you up."

"Cool, All I know is that Tristan stays in Hill Points."

Be ready bro we'll be there in about 15 minutes, later.

Nick accelerates the car and pulls a joint from the center console.

Nick fires up the joint and passes it to Jordan, "Yo hit that it will relax you."

Nick speeds through traffic and clarifies, "So this fool pulled a gun on you?"

Jordan hits the joint before replying, "Yeah I was dumping the trash out back when he and Tristan snuck me from behind. He pushed me down then drew down on me."

Nick's caught up in the story, "Then what happened?"

"My manager heard the noise and came back, that's when they took off."

Nick asks, "So did Tristan do anything?"

Jordan's phone buzzes. It's a text from his mom: *What time do you get off?*

He ignores it and puts it back in his pocket.

Nick approaches an intersection the light is yellow, he starts to slow down.

Jordan loudly yells, "Speed up you can make it! I need to see this fool tonight!"

Nick speeds up and the light turns red just as he is crossing the intersection.

Shooting through the intersection he has to brake suddenly to avoid rear-ending a gray Ford Explorer.

A cop at the stoplight sees this and immediately turns right and hits the lights.

Nick looks in his rearview mirror sees the police lights and yells, "Shit!"

Jordan turns around, "You think he is after us?"

"Who else would he be after? We just ran a red light, then almost had an accident." Nick yells.

Jordan suggests, "Maybe we can outrun him."

Nick looks in the rearview mirror the police car lights flashing directly behind them, "Fool are you serious? I'm not about to be in no police chase."

Jordan moans, "Dude we've been smoking weed. We going to be in a lot of trouble."

Nick still driving replies, "No shit bro, my only choice is to pull over."

Jordan panicky, "Just keep driving. Maybe we can get rid of the weed."

The police are directly behind them and he hits his siren button, making the whoop sound. Nick looks back and sees the policeman motioning him to pull over.

Jordan lets the window down exclaims, "Don't pull over yet. We need to get rid of the weed."

Nick looking in his rearview mirror says, "Look when I change lanes I'm going to pull in front of a car when I do you dump the weed then."

Nick continues driving. He speeds up and makes a quick change to the right lane in front of a blue Ford Mustang yells. "Now."

Jordan lets down the window and throws out the joint.

The police car speeds up and switches lanes in front of the same Mustang.

Nick takes a deep breath announces," I'm pulling over."

CHAPTER TWENTY-FIVE

Nick makes a right turn into a tire store parking lot, the police car follows directly behind them, lights still on.

The police officer sits in his car, talking on the radio.

Nick nervously, "I wonder what is taking him so long."

"You think he saw us dump the weed?" Jordan asks.

Nick replies, "I don't know bro, it seems like it's taking forever."

Nick looks at the outside car mirror and sees the policeman get out of his car, "He's coming up be cool, don't make any quick moves we don't want to be another unarmed black teenager getting shot by the police story."

The policeman approaches Nick's car with a flashlight in his left hand from the rear. He shines it in Jordan's face. He is a white officer about a 5'10" slim build with light brunette hair and a thin mustache, he appears to be in his early thirties.

He stops at Nick's door with his right hand resting on his gun says to him.

"Good evening. I'm Officer Corey Jackson, the reason I pulled you over was that you ran that light back there and almost caused an accident. Do you have your driver's license and proof of insurance?"

Nick looks up at the policeman. "I am reaching for my wallet to get my license." He then turns and grabs his wallet from his back pocket flips it open pulls out his license and hands it to the officer.

He then opens the center console. Right in plain sight are a pair of sunglasses, a small bag of weed, and the pistol magazine. Nick immediately closes it. He looks up at Jordan. His eyes widen with fear he then looks back at the cop who is still looking at Nick's license.

"So, do you have the car insurance or not?" Officer Jackson snaps.

Nick, flustered from the weed and magazine in the car, stammers, "I have to look a little bit more."

The cop says, "I'll be right back," and walks away to his police vehicle.

Nick looks in the rearview mirror and watches him get back into his patrol car.

Jordan asks, "Do you think he saw the weed and mag?"

Nick moans, "I don't know. I'm getting another ticket my grandad is going to kill me."

Another police car suddenly pulls into the parking lot and parks right beside the first police officer.

They both turn around and look at the two police cars.

Jordan mutters, "That's not good."

Jordan opens the glove box pulls out the gun and holds it down between his knees and asks, "So what are we supposed to do about this?"

Nick hisses, "Nigga is you stupid, put that shit back the cops right back there."

Jordan puts the gun back in the glove box, "Can we lock this?"

Nick sighs, "No it doesn't have a lock."

Jordan turned around looks out the window he warns, "Chill there both coming."

Both officers are walking with their flashlights out, Officer Jackson comes up to the driver's side. The second officer is a black man in his early thirties, chocolate brown muscular, bald about 6'2"he is wearing a super tight uniform to show off his body. He approaches the passenger side. He shines his flashlight all around the car but he stands back away from the car.

Officer Jackson asks Nick, "So were you able to find the insurance?"

Nick replies, "No officer."

"What about you do you have an ID?" he asks Jordan.

Jordan reaches in his back pocket and pulls out his license. He hands it to Officer Jackson.

He looks at them tells Jordan and Nick, "I need you both to step out of the car."

Nick becomes defensive asks, "Why? What did we do?"

The other officer from the other side, yells angrily, "You don't asks questions, just follow his instructions."

Jordan opens the passenger door, the officer tells them, "You sit over there," as he points at a spot on the parking lot ground.

Jordan defensively, "You want us to sit on the ground?"

The officer walks over to Jordan leans down whispers in his right ear, "Sit your ass down boy."

Jordan looks at him, shakes his head, and sits down, and the officer steps back behind them, Jordan, whispers, "Fucking sellout."

The officer walks up behind Jordan and inquires, "Did you say something?"

Jordan looks up at him and shakes his head and mutters, "Nothing man get away from me."

The officer grabs Jordan by his shoulder and yells, "On your feet."

Jordan caught off guard shrugs his arm to get away, and the police officer pushes him to the ground, he lands with a thud on his chest, the officer puts his right knee in his back, "Resisting arrest, I got you now." Jordan's on his stomach struggles to breathe as the policeman grabs his right arm and pulls it behind his back and puts on the handcuffs.

Nick sees this and jumps out of his car yells to Jordan, "Chill bro don't do anything stupid."

Officer Jackson to Nick, his right hand on his tazer, "You stay right there! Don't YOU do anything stupid!"

Jordan still lying on his stomach yells, "What I'd do? Why is he arresting me?"

"Be quiet," the officer demands as he is applying the second cuff. After the cuff is applied Jordan is rolled to his side and pulled up.

Officer Jackson orders Nick, "Go stand in front of the car."

Nick walks to the front of the car and asks, "Are you arresting me for not having my insurance?"

Officer Jackson walks up behind him and explains, "You are not being arrested for the insurance, I saw the weed and gun magazine in the car. Now place your hands on your head and interlock, your fingers. Do you have anything on you that can stick me?"

"Naw man," Nick answers dismissively.

Officer Jackson, pats him down, then places him in handcuffs.

Officer Jackson tells his partner, "Have him sit down by his friend. I'm going to search the vehicle."

Nick starts to squat to sit by Jordan he immediately stands back up and says loudly, "You can't search my vehicle without permission."

Officer Jackson puts on a pair of black gloves and explains from the other side of the car, "I don't need permission, with probable cause, the weed scent, pistol magazine that's all I need."

He opens the driver's door, immediately goes to the center console, and opens it up rummages around. He pulls out the loaded magazine and the bag of weed.

Officer Jackson says, "Looka here, looka here partner," dropping the bag of weed and the magazine on top of the car.

The other officer responds, "Jackpot! The only question now is the gun in the car?"

Jordan turns and looks nervously at Nick.

Officer Jackson sees this and nods, "Yep that's all I needed to see."

Nick turns to Jordan whispers, "Damn bro, be cool. Jordan fires back, "You really thought they weren't going to find it?"

Officer Jackson walks around the front of the car to the passenger side. Opens the door, then opens the glove box, and out drops the gun.

Both of them drop their head Jordan yells, "Fuck!"

The second officer walks behind Jordan, stands him up. "You got anything on you that you need to be worried about?"

Jordan angrily replies, "Fuck you."

"Keep talking," he says as he does a quick pat-down of Jordan.

Officer Jackson puts the items in plastic evidence bags, takes them to his patrol car places them in the front seat, he walks back over to them. He tells them, "You two are being placed under arrest for unlawful possession of a weapon and possession of an illegal substance. Alright let's go, I will take the driver."

The second officer responds, "Alright I got you," looks at Jordan, and tells him "Let's go."

Nick walking to the police car asks, "So what's going to happen to my car?"

The second officer replies, "It's going to the impound lot and see what other good stuff we can find. Alright, let's move."

CHAPTER TWENTY-SIX

Vicky's at home in the living room working on the puzzle with Ericka. She asks her, "So are you excited to see your dad tomorrow?"

Ericka's fiddling around with some puzzle pieces. She sighs, "I guess, do I have to go?"

Vicky sensing her sadness, "Me and your dad have an arrangement, you spend the summers with him, and I want to honor that because he loves you the same as I do."

Ericka sighs, "I know, I just hate Brooke. She is so annoying."

Vicky laughs, "She is your baby sister. You know that's what KJ and Jordan say about you," she teases as she looks at her cell phone. "Jordan is normally off already. Maybe he caught a ride with his friends."

She texts him: *Are you off yet?*

She puts the phone down and picks up a puzzle piece and continues the conversation with Ericka, "It's only for the summer and it will give us a chance to miss you."

Ericka nods, "Okay, so what time do I leave?"

"Your father texted me he's coming at nine tomorrow morning." She looks at her phone, Jordan still hasn't texted back.

She grabs her phone and stands up. "Let's go."

"Where are we going?" Ericka stands up and follows her.

"We're going to check on Jordan something doesn't feel right."

The two police officers pull into the Allen County Juvenile Detention parking lot.

Officer Jackson opens the door and lets Jordan out of the backseat, he yells over to the other policeman. "Yo Smitty, let's hurry up and get them in I'm hungry."

"All right bet. I'm guessing yours works at the Burger House with that uniform on. Maybe we can stop by there and get something to eat before they close."

Officer Jackson approaches the detention center, with both boys in the middle and Officer Smith in the back. He rings the buzzer and a voice on the intercom answers, "Yes?"

"It's Officer Jackson. I got two to drop off."

The intercom voice replies, "Hold on," the door buzzes open. Officer Jackson pulls open the door and motions the teens to enter. Once inside there is a holding area and another door with another buzzer. Officer Jackson hears the click and opens that door.

Once inside there is a desk where the detention supervisor is sitting. On the right side of the desk, there is a white bench about 10 feet long. The supervisor from behind the desk points to the bench and tells Nick and Jordan, "Sit down here."

Officer Smith asks, "So where is the bathroom?" The detention officer stands up and points. "Go down and make a left the staff bathroom is on the right." He walks hurriedly down the hall.

Detention Supervisor Reed sits back down tells Officer Jackson, "I will need you to sign them in. So, what'd you get them on?"

Officer Jackson replies, "Possession of an illegal substance and illegal firearm he points at Jordan adds, "This one also has a resisting arrest." Supervisor Reed states, "I need to finish these forms, if you want to help you can uncuff them."

Officer Smith has returned just in time to hear the request. He walks to Jordan and orders him, "On your feet." He stands up and is uncuffed.

Officer Jackson asks, "Where do I sign? You can fill in the rest later, we need to be going we got our paperwork to do with the evidence we found."

Officer Jackson grabs the form, "Where do I sign?"

Supervisor Reed points to the bottom of the form, "Right here."

Officer Jackson grabs the paper and signs the forms. Reed pushes two more forms in front of him, he signs both of those. "Well if that's it we need to get going."

He looks back at them sitting on the bench," See you around," the door is buzzed and both officers leave.

Vicky turns into the Burger House, Ericka is asleep in the front seat, and KJ is in the back.

"Most of the lights are off, I think they are closed." KJ points out.

Vicky worried answers, "Yeah I texted your brother, I got no answer."

She drives around to the drive-through. The menu sign is dark, but she drives up to the window nobody is there so she blows the horn. The manager Mark comes to the window, "I'm sorry ma'am we are closed."

Vicky explains, "I am not here to get something to eat. I'm looking for my son, Jordan is he here?"

"Uh he was here but he left about an hour ago without clocking out."

Vicky surprised asks, "Left? With who?"

Mark replies, "I'm not sure, he was taking the trash out back and something happened out there. When I asked him what happened, he just stormed off. He left without finish cleaning up. About 15 minutes later some other boy came and picked him up."

"Something happened out back? What does that mean?"

"I don't know, he just came back from dumping trash pisssed, he didn't talk to me, hold on, Brittany come here. Did Jordan tell you what happened out back?"

She looks nervously at Mark and stammers, "He had a gun pulled on him."

KJ hears this and sits up in the back.

Vicky demands, "What are you talking about?"

Brittany looks at Vicky and says, "He was dumping trash and some boy pulled a gun on him."

Vicky excitedly asks, "Did he say who? Why? Where did he go?"

Brittany overwhelmed with all the questions, shakes her head. "I don't know anything but what I just told you." She walks away in a hurry.

Mark looks at Vicky apologizes, "I'm sorry we couldn't be more help," he closes the window.

She drives off, KJ excitedly asks, "I can't believe, somebody pulled a gun on Jordan. You think he went to shoot him?"

Vicky in her head is wondering the same question as she drives out of the parking lot, "I don't know, with his attitude lately, I wouldn't be surprised," She drives around wondering about her next move. "Do you know where his friends live at?"

KJ on his phone, "Hold up mom I'm calling Jordan,"

The phone rings without no answer and goes straight to voice mail, he hangs up. Vicky shakes her head worriedly asks again, "Do you know where his friends live?"

"No."

She takes a deep breath. "Maybe they went back to Keith's house, I'd better go check."

She makes a U-turn, her phone rings the caller ID reads, "Allen County Juvenile Detention Center."

Vicky looks at her phone thinks, *This can't be good,* she takes a deep breath answers,

"Hello?"

"This is Supervisor Reed at the Allen County Juvenile Detention, I'm calling to let you know your son Jordan has been arrested and is here at our facility."

Vicky not totally surprised, *"Please don't tell, me he's shot, somebody."*

Officer Reed quickly assures her, *"No it's nothing that serious, he was arrested with another boy, they had some weed and a gun in the car, also your son was charged with resisting arrest."*

Vicky takes a deep breath and sighs, *"I don't believe this first his father then him, what's the saying 'like father like son."*

Reed chuckles a little at the joke before replying, *"Um Ok."*

Vicky driving home asks, *"So when will I get a chance to talk to him?"*

"Right now he is in a holding cell waiting to be processed in, if he doesn't call you tonight he should be able tomorrow morning."

Vicky dejectedly," *Thank you, goodnight.*" She hangs up and shakes her head.

KJ leans forward and asks, "Is Jordan in jail?"

Vicky without answering nods her head.

CHAPTER TWENTY-SEVEN

The next morning Jordan and Nick are in the day area of the detention center sitting at a table.

Jordan snarls, "That resisting arrest charge was bullshit."

Nick complains "That whole stop was bullshit, they didn't have the right to search my car."

Detention Officer Kenneth Bruton, behind the control desk, stands up and asks loudly, "Is there anyone who wants to make a phone call?"

Both of them raise their hand, Bruton adds, "If you just came in last night, and didn't get a phone call stand up." They both stand up.

Mr. Bruton points at them says, "You two come up here, and take a seat." He points to a table with 4 phones on them.

Both of them get up and go to the table and sit down in front of the phones.

Officer Bruton looks at Nick, "Who do you want to call?"

Nick answers, "My grandmother."

Officer Bruton shuffles through some papers, then starts dialing. He tells Nick, "It's ringing pick it up you got 5 minutes."

Officer Bruton asks Jordan, "Who are you calling?"

Jordan sits there and answers, "My mom."

Bruton shuffles through some papers again, dials the number, and tells Jordan, "Pick it up it's ringing, you got 5 minutes."

Jordan stares at the phone takes a deep breath and picks it up.

Vicky's in the kitchen, making breakfast for Ericka and KJ when her phone rings. She picks it up off the counter, looks at the caller ID. Then looks at Ericka and KJ, she says, "It's probably your brother."

Vicky answers, "Hello?"

Jordan in a low tone, "Hi mom, I got arrested last night."

Vicky sighs, "Yeah they called. So, what happened?"

Jordan explains, "Last night at work this fool, pulled a gun on me, Nick came and picked me up, and...

Vicky interrupts him, "So what were you going to do when you saw him?"

Jordan speaks a little louder, "I don't know, but I ain't no punk."

Vicky angrily asks, "What does that even mean? 'I ain't no punk?' All you have to show for it is your ass is locked up now."

Jordan getting frustrated whines, "The police pushed me on the ground and I got a bruise on my chest and you don't even care."

Vicky cries, "What?? I don't care?" If I didn't care I wouldn't be talking to you now, I wouldn't have sent you to your father's place. I wouldn't be dealing with all your drama."

Jordan murmurs, "I could have been killed."

Vicky's voice grows louder with emotion, "You don't think I know that? That boy who pulled the gun out at your job could have shot you. Then the police pull you over, they shoot black men like there is a hunting season for them. Do not give them a reason to even think you're a threat, you know this. You hear the news."

Jordan asks, "So what's going to happen to me?"

Vicky replies, "I honestly don't know."

In the background, Mr. Bruton calls out, "You got 1-minute left."

Vicky hears this and tells him, "Well I got to get Ericka ready for her dad."

Jordan asks, "So that's this weekend? Tell her I said be good and I'll see her soon."

Vicky sighs, "I'm try and come see you when I can, you be good, love you son."

Jordan responds "Love you, mom. Bye."

At 9 a.m. Monday at the detention center, Jordan and Nick are sitting in the day area playing cards. A black woman in her mid-thirties walks in caring a computer tablet, and a folder full of papers. She walks into the room and sits at a table in the corner by herself. Supervisor Reed comes to the table and they talk quietly.

Jordan has his back to them, Nick looks at them asks, "I wonder what they are talking about?"

Jordan turns around looks, "I don't know bro, probably us. Play your card."

They continue playing cards. After 7 minutes, Supervisor Reed stands up and calls out, "Jordan can you come here?"

Jordan surprised walks over to the table. Officer Reed to Jordan, "Take a seat, this is Mrs. Butler and she is going to be your probation officer."

Jordan sits down, Mrs. Butler opens up the folder, "I've been reading up on your case, you want to tell me what happened?"

Jordan begins, "Well me and my bro Nick were riding in his car, and the police said we ran a light so they pulled us over, then another cop pulls up and makes us get out of the car, they search the car illegally, the other cop pushes me on the ground and bruises up my chest." He then pulls up his orange uniform top and shows a black circular bruise about 6 inches round on the right side by his rib cage.

Mrs. Butler calmly asks, "Is that it? Did you tell me everything?"

Jordan pulls his shirt down, "Yeah."

Mrs. Butler comments, "Well according to the police report, y'all had weed and a gun in the car. What do you have to say about that?"

Jordan fidgets in the chair, "Well there was some weed, but we weren't smoking it when they saw us, the gun's not mine I don't know anything about that."

Mrs. Butler inquires, "If the gun is not yours then why are your fingerprints on it?"

Jordan anxiously answers, "Well I did hold it, just to see what it felt like, but I wasn't the only one to hold it."

Mrs. Butler responds, "I am your probation officer, so you are the only one I am concerned with, and if this is going to work I need you to be totally honest with me."

Jordan says, "So what is going to happen to me?"

Mrs. Butler explains, "This could play out a few different ways, I don't want to say too much until I get some more information. It all depends what charges they pursue, you could be looking at some felonies."

Jordan drops his head.

Mrs. Butler adds, "I need to speak with your mother to discuss the situation with her to see what she thinks."

Jordan discloses, "I've already talked with her and she doesn't believe me either."

Mrs. Butler suggests, "If you want people to believe you then start being truthful with them."

Jordan asks, "Can I go?"

Mrs. Butler answers, "Yes, I will be getting back to you later this week."

CHAPTER TWENTY-EIGHT

Reign walks up to the door and rings the bell.

KJ answers it, Reign says, "I'm sorry, I was wondering does Jordan Skyy live here?"

KJ answers, "Yeah he does but he is not here."

Vicky walks in from the kitchen and asks, "KJ who is it?"

KJ responds, "I don't know it's a girl asking for Jordan."

Vicky reaches the door and states, "Oh ok your Jordan's friend..."

"Reign."

Vicky smiles at her, "I'm sorry we never actually met, but I remember you dropped him off here about three weeks ago, come in."

Reign walks in, and all three go to the couch. Reign sits in the middle with KJ to her right.

Reign tells her, "I'm sorry to just drop by but I haven't heard from Jordan for about two weeks. Is everything alright with him?"

Vicky sighs, "He got arrested about two weeks ago."

"Oh, no! I would have come by sooner, but we were busy moving last week."

Vicky inquires, "Oh really. So where did you move to?"

Reign answers, "Just down the street, I thought Jordan would have told you. You said he was arrested so what happened?"

Vicky sits up on the couch and takes a deep breath. "Well, he and his friend were driving and got pulled over by the police. They had some weed and a gun in the car."

Reign leans forward shocked, "A gun!"

"Jordan says he was at work and some boy came up there and pulled a gun on him, and he was trying to find him when they got pulled over by the cops."

Reign hears this and wonders, *Damn! Did DJ pull a gun on him?*

Vicky continues, "He says he is doing okay; I'm try and visit him this weekend."

Reign stands up and shakily says, "I've got to be going tell Jordan when you see him that I asked about him."

Vicky stands up, "Well thank you for stopping by, and nice to actually meet you." She extends her arms and they hug.

Reign walks to the door and turns around and asks, "Is it ok if I stop by sometimes to see how he is doing?"

Vicky smiles, "Sure honey anytime, I think he will like hearing that you asked about him."

Vicky pulls into the Allen County Juvenile Detention. The parking lot is quite full she ends up parking on the far end of the lot a 10-minute walk away from the detention center. Before she gets out she leaves her phone in the glove box.

She walks in and there is a line of six people ahead of her, when she gets to the front the female officer asks without looking up, "Name and government ID"

Vicky reaches into her jeans front pocket and pulls out her driver's license.

She looks at the license then looks at Vicky, "Ok sign here," as she slides a piece of paper in front of her.

After signing it, she hands Vicky a sheet of paper saying, "Here are the rules. You can have a seat."

Vicky goes to sit down and after a 20-minute wait, her name is called. She goes back behind a locked door and inside is the day area with four 10-foot square tables with 4 blue chairs on each side one side seats the juveniles the other visitors.

A guard escorts Vicky to an empty table in the corner, and Vicky takes a seat. The officer says, "Jordan will be here shortly." He then goes and stands next to the wall.

Jordan comes into the room and looks around when he sees Vicky a big smile comes across his face he walks over to the table, she stands up excited to see him and they hug. The officer walks over, "I'm sorry you're not allowed to embrace."

Vicky immediately let's go. "I'm sorry this is just our first time seeing each other since he got locked up."

They both sit down Vicky asks, "So how are you doing?"

Jordan replies, "Good."

Vicky tells him, "Your friend, Reign stopped by earlier this week to asks about you."

Jordan excited to hear this, "Really? So, what did she say?"

Vicky continues, "Not too much really. She told me her family moved to a house down the street from us, and that since she hadn't heard from you, she decided to stop by."

Jordan smile says, "That's what's up."

Vicky asks, "So you and her going out?"

Jordan smiles slowly disappears, "We were. I really don't know what's going to happen now."

Vicky reassures him. "I wouldn't worry about it I can tell she likes you."

Jordan excitedly asks, "Did she say something?"

Vicky smiles at Jordan's excitement. "No, a mother just knows." She takes a more serious tone, "So have you heard any more about your case?"

Jordan explains, "I talked to my probation officer and she told me that I'm probably either get probation or boot camp."

Vicky nods in agreement, "I talked to her and she told me the same thing. Well, the good news is it could be only 3 months if you go to boot camp."

Jordan complains, "I don't want to go to boot camp for no months. Can't you get me a lawyer?"

Vicky sighs, "Your dad is pressuring me about a lawyer and now you too. You know I can't afford a lawyer, you need to look at the big picture, they got your fingerprints on the gun, they found weed in the car, and your urine test came back hot. Mrs. Butler told me you would be getting a big break if you only get 3 months. So why were you holding the gun anyway?"

Jordan, "I don't know it was in the car and I just grabbed it wanting to see what it felt like, then the cops pulled us over.

Vicky shakes her head. "You didn't think to wipe the gun off?"

Jordan stammers, "I was scared I wasn't thinking."

Vicky declares, "Now you're set up to take the fall for a gun that's not yours. Why don't you tell them it's Nick's gun?"

Jordan, "What? I can't snitch on him. That's my fam. This is the way it fell I just got to roll with it."

Vicky shakes her head again, "I just don't understand this blind loyalty to take the fall for something you didn't do."

Jordan sighs, "That's just the way it is mom. He would do the same for me." He attempts to change the subject. "I told you the police pushed me. What about that?"

"They are saying you were resisting arrest and he did it for officer safety."

Jordan angrily protests, "That's bullshit, that cop was just an asshole."

Vicky shakes her head again, "That's probably true, but it's your word versus them who do you think they're going to believe."

Jordan sits there quietly head down.

Vicky grabs his chin and holds his head up, "Don't you hold your head down. We are not beaten we can get through this."

Jordan looks at her, "You right," and takes a deep breath, "So how's KJ and Ericka?"

Vicky replies, "It's just me and KJ until school starts, you know Ericka is with her dad until school starts back."

Jordan asks, "So where is KJ?"

"Since this was the first visit, I wanted to come by myself, he is with his friend Dre until I come home."

Jordan, "Tell him I said what's up."

The officer comes to the table and leans down, "Y'all got 5 minutes."

Vicky looks up at him, "Thank you." She turns to Jordan, "Your probation officer is supposed to call me sometime this week to let me know about your court date."

Jordan asks, "You coming back next week?"

Vicky stands up, "I should be able to, I'll see if I can bring KJ next time."

Jordan smiles, "That would be cool."

He stands up, they both look at the detention officer he turns his head and they do a quick hug. Just before they let go Vicky looks him in the face tells him, "Three months, you need to seriously think about that."

Jordan looks at her, "All right mom, I'll think about it. Love You."

"Love you too, Jordan."

CHAPTER TWENTY-NINE

Vicky is at work at the Erving Memorial Hospital. She is about to enter a patient's room when her phone rings. She pulls it out of her light pink nurse scrub top, looks at it, it's the Allen County Juvenile Detention, she pushes the button to ignore the call.

Instead of going into the room, she turns around and walks back to the nurse station.

Kelly another nurse is there. Vicky pulls out her phone and asks her, "Can you check on room six? I just got a phone call I need to take."

Kelly says, "Alright, is everything ok?"

Vicky shakes her head no, "Not really, but you have to roll with it." She walks away and goes to the break room and takes a seat and redials.

"Hello, my name is Vicky Skyy, and someone just called me."

The receptionist responds, "Please hold for a second."

Vicky finds herself listening to some elevator music.

Finally, after a long three minutes wait a woman's voice comes on, "Hi I'm Mrs. Audrey Butler, and we spoke about a week ago.

Vicky asks, "So you were the one who called me ten minutes ago?"

Mrs. Butler confirms, "Yes I want to update you about Jordan's case. He has a court date in two weeks."

Vicky says, "That's pretty fast."

Mrs. Butler asks, "Will you be able to be there?"

"Of course, so what do you think is going to happen?"

Mrs. Butler speculates, "Well based on the police reports and all the information I have, he could get probation or an indeterminate sentence at the boot camp."

Vicky inquires, "So based on your experiences what do you think will happen?"

Mrs. Butler states, "He should get probation. Do you have a lawyer?"

Vicky sighs "No, I can't afford one."

Mrs. Butler sympathizes, "I understand. Then he will get a public defender. So, have you had a chance to see Jordan?"

Vicky replies, "Yeah I saw him this past weekend. He is doing ok under the circumstance."

Mrs. Butler explains, "When you hear from the public defender, we all need to have a meeting."

Vicky agrees, "Okay, I will call you when I hear something."

Reign's in her new bedroom, sitting at her desk, phone in her hand thinking about whether she should call Dejuan or not. Finally, she decides, *fuck it,* and calls him.

The phone rings and he answers immediately. "What's up girl? Good hearing from you."

Reign snaps, "I'm not here to talk to you socially, I need to asks did you pull a gun on Jordan at his job?"

DJ exclaims, "What?? What are you talking about?"

Reign responds, "So you don't know anything about somebody pulling a gun on Jordan about a month ago."

DJ swears, "No I don't know anything about what you're talking about. What happened?"

Reign is still very skeptical, "Somebody pulled a gun on him at work, when he went after him the cops pulled him and his friend over."

DJ excitedly asks, "So he got arrested?"

Reign sighs, "Yeah he is locked up."

DJ sarcastically answers, "Man that is so fucked up." He takes his shot, "So what's up? You think we can get back together?"

Reign laughs humorously, "Are you serious right now? How stupid are you? I just call to see if you were the one who pulled the gun on Jordan. Just so you know I don't believe you. First, you threatened him on Instagram then you stalking me at my house.

I know it was you, if I find out you did it, I will never forgive you."

DJ angrily yells, "Don't call me stupid. I don't care if you forgive me or not, we are not going out. If I pulled a gun on your boyfriend, I'd smoke that fool." He hangs up.

CHAPTER THIRTY

Vicky drives home from work, when her phone rings, it's from the Allen County Juvenile, she answers it. "Hello."

"Yes, this is Mrs. Butler, has the public defender reached out to you yet?"

Vicky replies, "Yes I talked with him a few days ago."

Mrs. Butler explains, "Well he got back with me and would like to meet tomorrow, to go over everything before we go to trial next week. What time would be good for you?"

Vicky states, "I wish you would have called earlier." She pauses, "Can we do it during my lunch hour from, 1130 to 1230?"

Mrs. Butler silent for a few seconds answers, "We will make it work. See you tomorrow."

Vicky, Jordan, and Mrs. Butler are sitting in a conference room at the Allen County Juvenile Detention Center. Vicky looks at the clock on the wall it's 11:40.

Vicky anxiously asks, "Do you know what's going on?"

Mrs. Butler replies, "I don't know I tried calling him and it went straight to voice mail."

A tall slim black man with a bald head and a smoothly shaved goatee wearing some black slacks a black golf shirt and matching black square-toed loafers walks into the conference room, carrying some folders and a tablet, he drops them on the table, "I'm sorry about being late court ran a little long, I'm Mitchell Legette."

Vicky stands up and shakes his hand then Jordan does the same.

Mr. Legette takes a seat beside Vicky; Jordan takes a seat on the other side.

Mr. Legette begins speaking, "Well I looked at your case and after reviewing the files, I would like to asks how do you plan on pleading?"

Vicky asks, "What are his choices?"

Mr. Legette explains, "He has three choices Not guilty, Guilty, or Nolo Contendere which means no contest. You are not admitting guilt or innocence, but the court treats it as a guilty plea."

Jordan declares, "I'm not pleading guilty I know that."

Vicky inquires, "So what's the benefit of him pleading nolo contendere?"

Mr. Legette clarifies, "Well if he pleads guilty, he loses the right to appeal, if he pleads nolo contendere, he can appeal later but only if he points out what he believes was a mistake during his trial."

Vicky asks, "So what do you believe is his best option?"

Mr. Legette explains, "I'm not at liberty to tell you how to plead that is a decision that you and Jordan have to make, ultimately it's Jordan's, but I can tell you I believe I can get him probation based on what I see from the reports."

Jordan hears this and drops his head, "I don't want no damn probation,"

Mr. Legette tells him, "Under the circumstance you would be very fortunate, to get probation."

Vicky turns to Jordan, "That's what we been telling him."

Mr. Legette looks at Jordan, "Tell me why you think you shouldn't get probation?"

Jordan snaps, "The police harassed us and threw me on the ground for no reason."

Mr. Legette responds, "Yes I read your complaint, but the police counter by accusing you of becoming aggressive after getting out of the car and he took you down for his safety."

Jordan cries, "Why doesn't anyone believe me?"

Mr. Legette leans over and looks directly at Jordan. "Just look at the circumstances, you got 2 black teenagers, who get pulled over for running a red light and almost having an accident. The police find weed and a handgun with the serial number scratched off in the car, and then your fingerprints are found on the gun. Those are felony charges. You are a black man in America. Who do you think they are going to believe you or the police?"

Jordan sits there with his head down, Vicky comments, "What did I tell you about putting your head down?"

Vicky inquires, "Ok so what's our next move?"

Mr. Legette responds, "Hopefully I can get the charges dropped to a misdemeanor with this being his first arrest. He hasn't had any trouble here in detention, so all this is good. Probation should probably be no more than 2 years tops, and if it goes well, it might get dropped even sooner. Well if there are no more questions, I got another case at one." He stands up, "I'm trying to squeeze in a lunch."

Vicky takes a deep breath, "Okay I need to get back to work myself."

Mr. Legette looks at Jordan and tells him, "I will see you in court Monday. He looks at Vicky, "Will you be able to make it?"

Vicky matter of factly, "Of course that's my baby, I'm going to be with him every step of the way."

Monday morning Jordan and Nick are in the dayroom, playing dominos.

Nick looks at the dayroom wall clock. "It's 8:15," he inquires, "I thought you had court today at nine?"

Jordan replies, "I do."

Nick asks, "So are you nervous?"

Jordan retorts, "Hell yeah, I got a felony hanging over my head?"

Nick takes a deep breath, "Look bro straight up I appreciate you not snitching on me about the piece."

Jordan looks at him, "You my boy, and I wouldn't do that, I know you would do the same for me right?"

"Of course, bro," he assures Jordan. They dap each other up.

Jordan teases, "You owe me for this fool."

Detention Officer Bruton steps into the day area looks at Jordan yells, "Skyy come on let's go you got court in 35 minutes.

Jordan gets up, Nick stands up they bro-hug each other. Nick, "Good luck J."

Jordan, "Thanks bro, I'll see you later."

Jordan's handcuffed and leg shackled and escorted into the courtroom by Officer Bruton. He comes in through a side door. The bailiff is already standing by the judge's bench. The courtroom is empty except for his mother, sitting in the front row behind his public defender, Mr. Legette. On the other side is another man sitting at a table. Mr. Bruton stops him in front of the table tells him, "I'm going to release your hands, take a seat by your lawyer, and don't cause any problems."

Jordan nods says, "Okay."

After sitting down, next to Mr. Legette, Vicky leans up and touches his right shoulder he looks back at her and smiles.

Mr. Legette asks, "Are you nervous?"

Jordan shakes his head yes.

Mr. Legette assures him, "That's to be expected, just follow my instructions and everything will be fine.

The judge walks into the courtroom, the bailiff calls out loudly, "All rise for the Honorable Vincent Brown." Everybody stands up. The judge does a scan of the room and says, "You may be seated."

The judge speaks very loudly, "We are here for the adjudication hearing of Jordan Skyy, for the charges of possession of a controlled substance and illegal possession of a handgun and resisting arrest." He looks at the table, "How does the defendant plea?"

Mr. Legette stands up and states, "He pleads nolo contendere."

The judge writes on a paper then says, "The defendant has entered a plea of no contest. Does the defendant understand this plea?" He asks Jordan who shakes his head yes.

Judge Brown says, "I need you to verbally speak it so it can be entered into the court record."

Jordan responds, "Yes sir."

The judge continues. "If the state is ready, we can begin."

The prosecuting attorney stands up and asks, "Could you give us a few minutes my witnesses are on their...

The court doors open, and the police officers walk in.

CHAPTER THIRTY-ONE

The two police officers walk into the court and take a seat with the prosecuting attorney, he looks at Judge Brown, "Could you get me a minute while I conference with these officers."

Judge Brown replies, "You have 2 minutes."

Jordan nervously asks Mr. Legette, "Did you know they were going to be here today?"

Vicky leans in to hear the conversation.

Mr. Legette whispers, "Yes, keep your cool, we will be all right."

Jordan inquires, "So why didn't you tell me?"

Mr. Legette whispers, "Because I didn't want this reaction right here pull yourself together. It will be alright."

Jordan sits back in the chair and slouches down. Vicky taps him on the shoulder signals him to sit up.

The attorney stands up and announces, "Judge we're ready."

Judge Brown strikes the gavel. "Court is now in session. The prosecution may proceed."

The attorney gets up walks around the table and states, "I would like Officer Corey Jackson to take the stand." The officer gets up and walks to the stand and is sworn in by the bailiff.

"Officer Jackson could you tell us about the incident on the night of June 26 that led up to the arrest of the defendant."

Officer Jackson testifies, "I was on routine patrol and was stopped at the traffic light at Camden and 24th street, I observed a gray Honda accord at a high rate of speed. The driver ran the red traffic light, then had to brake hard to avoid having a rear-end collision with a white Ford Explorer. I turned on 24$^{th\ street}$ and hit the lights. I initially thought the vehicle was trying to elude me."

The attorney asks, "Then what happened?"

"I pursued the vehicle until the driver pulled into a parking lot and stopped. I called the tag number to check if the car had been reported stolen. Then I went to the vehicle and asked for the driver's license and insurance. Nick Graham was the driver, and the defendant was in the passenger seat. When I approached the vehicle, I immediately noticed the aroma of marijuana coming from the car."

Jordan shakes his head no and cries, "That's a lie."

Judge Brown looks at him and in a serious voice, "You need to be quiet young man."

Officer Jackson continues, "Well after getting Mr. Graham's license I went back to my patrol car and called for backup before I proceeded any further. After Officer Smith arrived, he and I proceeded to the vehicle. Where we identified the defendant as Jordan Skyy. Due to the aroma coming from the car, I proceeded to have the driver step out of the car and Officer Smith ordered the defendant to get out of the car he was highly agitated and became aggressive. Officer Smith had to physically restrain him."

Jordan slams his hand on the table yells, "He's fucking lying! He threw me on the ground causes he's a racist asshole cop."

The judge admonishes Mr. Legette, "You need to tell the defendant that he is not helping his case with these emotional outbursts."

Mr. Legette pleads with Jordan, "Control yourself son."

Vicky leans forward and whispers in his ear, "What in the hell are you doing, you are about to ruin any chance you have of getting probation."

Jordan shrugs her off and looks at Mr. Legette. "You are just going to sit there and let them tell lies, and not do anything?"

Mr. Legette replies, "Calm down. You will get your chance to tell your side."

Jordan shouts, "This is such bullshit."

Judge Brown bangs the gavel three times looks at the detention officer Mr. Bruton tells him, "I've heard enough, could you cuff him and remove him from my court."

Vicky sits there stunned. She puts her face in her hands and starts to cry.

Officer Bruton stands up approaches Jordan, shaking his head, "Put your hands behind your back. You just blew it, son."

Jordan breathing hard still emotionally charged up puts his hands behind his back and is cuffed.

Judge Brown looks at Jordan and raises his voice to get his attention. "I just want to say this to you son before you leave, based on the information I had concerning the case you probably would have received probation. However, due to your outburst, it seems like you have no respect for authority. A residential placement may be the place where you can learn some respect and self-control. You are getting an indeterminate sentence to the Allen County Juvenile Bootcamp, hopefully where you'll learn some respect and improve your attitude. Take him outta here."

"Fuck You Judge," he yells out as Officer Bruton walks him out.

CHAPTER THIRTY-TWO

Jordan's back at the detention center; the residents are all in the day area watching a movie on a flat-screen TV. After being released from the cuffs he goes and takes a seat beside Joey Waddles a kid who is waiting to go to boot camp.

"So where is Nick?" Jordan asks.

Joey replies, "I don't know he left about 15 minutes after you did. So, what happened?"

Jordan moans, "It wasn't good. I'm going to boot camp."

Joey excited to hear this, "Cool bro, will be down there together."

Jordan mutters, "Whatever bro, I wasn't trying to go, I fucked up and went off, now I'm going there for I don't know how long."

Joey explains, "I'm good with it bro, I had 3 felonies that got reduced so I can go to boot camp I was looking at least 2 years. I'm good with 6 months in boot camp."

Jordan sarcastically, "Good for you."

Nick comes through the same door that he was taken through to go to court, he is with his grandparents and his probation officer.

He looks at Jordan, and is smiling, Jordan wonders, *Why is he happy?*

They all go into an office; the probation officer shuts the door.

Jordan turns back around and asks Joey, "I wonder what is going on with him?"

Joey suggests, "Maybe he is going home."

Jordan shakes his head no, "Naw that can't be right."

They both continue watching the movie. After fifteen minutes Nick comes from the office and shuts the door.

Jordan turns around and gestures for Nick to come over. Nick walks over and squats down in front of him.

Jordan asks, "What's going on?"

Nick says excitedly, "I got probation I'm outta here."

Jordan equally excited, "What? How?"

Nick explains, "Well my lawyer had a detention hearing, with the probation department and he was able to get the weed charge dismissed and the weapons charge wasn't on me so I just got the driving without insurance which I have to pay a fine on and I got a year of probation.

Jordan hears this and he gets a little angry, "Yo that gun ain't even mine, that's BS!"

Nick attempts to keep cool, "So what happened in court with you?"

Jordan complains, "The police showed up and lied about me resisting arrest I got pissed and the judge sent me to boot camp."

The probation officer steps out and sees Nick, talking to Jordan. "Mr. Graham you need to get going, your family is waiting.

Nick stands up says, "Aight bro I got to go."

Jordan stands up and gives him a bro hug and replies, "I'll see you around."

Jordan is experiencing mixed feelings. He's happy that Nick is going home, pissed he is going to boot camp on a gun charge that is not even his.

A couple of days later, Jordan is handcuff and sitting on the bench in front of the detention intake desk with Officer Bruton behind the desk.

The boot camp Juvenile Supervision Officer (JSO for short) comes in through the door. JSO Bentley is a 5'8" white male clean-shaven, about 25-30 with a blond hair cut in the military high and tight style. He's wearing the Bootcamp uniform of a black t-shirt, black cargo pants, and black combat boots.

Officer Bruton greets him, "What's up Bentley?"

Bentley answers back, "What's up Bruton? Is this Skyy?"

"Yeah, all the forms have been filled out I just need you to sign in the marked spots."

JSO Bentley answers, "Cool. Does he have any meds?"

Officer Bruton replies, "No but these are his clothes," He's patting a clear plastic bag sitting on the desk.

Bentley signs the forms, looks at Jordan, and orders, "On your feet."

Jordan stands up and Bentley grabs the bag of clothes and shoves it in Jordan's stomach, "Carry your stuff, let's go."

The Allen County Juvenile Bootcamp is on the other side they are connected through an enclosed chain link walkway. While walking down the sidewalk JSO Bentley tells Jordan in a serious tone, "I'm JSO Bentley the first and last words out of your mouth when you speak to staff is sir or ma'am. Do you understand?"

Jordan nervously answers, "Sir yes sir."

JSO Bentley, "You need to say it where I can hear you. Stop sounding like a little girl."

Jordan a little louder "Sir yes sir."

JSO Bentley shakes his head, "Will get you there."

Once they come through the fenced-in sidewalk there is a 25-foot high fence with sharp concertina wire at the top that is wrapped around the entire 100,000 square feet of property. Across the big open field is an off-white concrete building, to their left is another building, JSO Bentley points to the building on the left says, "This way."

JSO Bentley explains, "Anytime staff is approaching a building you need to hold the door open."

Jordan shuffles to the door and pulls it open.

JSO Bentley comments, "Good job," and shakes his head approvingly.

They walk inside and it is a brightly painted white with a highly shined wax floor with two offices beside each other and two small empty rooms next to each other.

JSO Bentley grabs the bag from Jordan and points to the empty room, "You need to step in there I will get your case manager so she can start the intake paperwork."

Jordan follows his instructions and stands against the wall, Bentley shuts the door.

Bentley goes into one of the offices, an older black female is sitting at a desk, He tells her, "Your intake is here."

She stands up and grabs some forms, and gives Bentley some boot camp clothes, "Here change him into these. So, how was he?"

Bentley replies, "No problems, you can tell he's nervous."

Mrs. Roebuck responds, "Hopefully that holds out I heard he acted a fool in court, that's why he's here. Well go ahead and do the scars and tattoos and have him change over."

Bentley walks over and opens the door, suddenly there is a commotion in a classroom, and desks are being pushed around some residents are yelling, "Fight Fight!"

Bentley shuts the door and tells Jordan, "Don't you go anywhere."

He runs to the other side there are 2 kids on the teacher's desk fighting, a white male JSO about 5'10" bald head with a blond goatee looking a lot like the wrestler Goldberg, except shorter, is attempting to break up the fight. Once they roll off the desk and onto the floor Bentley grabs one of the kids. JSO Ashley has the other kid pinned against the whiteboard, and he is struggling to break free. JSO Ashley leans into him with some extra force, tells him, "The more you resist the longer I'm going to keep you restrained." The kid is a Hispanic about 15 years old says, "Let me go bitch!" Ashley still in control says calmly, "Not going to happen until you relax." JSO Bentley takes his kid outside the classroom, pinning him against the wall says to him, "It's over calm down." The resident a light-skinned black kid also about age fifteen says, "I'm good."

Suddenly three other JSO's arrive, Sgt. Crawford yells, "They're both going to the brig." Bentley still has the resident pinned to the wall asks, "You good?"

He yells back at Bentley, "I said I was!"

JSO Bentley relaxes but still maintains control.

"Alright, you know you have to go to the brig until we find out what's going on."

"Yeah, I'm BTA when you dis my set," he yells as he is being escorted by Bentley.

The Hispanic kid hearing this yells, "Fuck you and your set."

They walk past, Jordan still in the room, the kid looks at Jordan as he is being escorted out. Jordan thinks to himself, *"What kind of place is this?"*

CHAPTER THIRTY-THREE

Jordan has been in this room for almost an hour he sits down on the floor, back on the wall, a different JSO comes and opens the door, with a booming voice says, "On your feet Recruit."

Jordan immediately stands up. They walk out the door across the big open field.

"I'm JSO Towers he is another white male about 6'4" with short brown hair about 40 years old clean-shaven with a small scar on his right chin smelling like cigarettes tells Jordan in a gravelly voice, "I'm doing your intake now, and I don't have a lot of time to explain everything to you. We are going down to the barracks to cut your hair, shave, shower, and change you over to the boot camp uniform. I will have a senior cadet explain the ins and outs of the daily program to you. What you don't learn today you will tomorrow, we pretty much do the same thing every day anyway, you understand?"

Jordan mumbles, "Yeah."

Towers stops him in the field, "I know you were instructed the first and last words out of your mouth were sir. "

Jordan loudly, "Sir yes sir."

Towers steps real close to Jordan looks down at him with a scowl says, "Am I detecting some attitude from you boy?"

Jordan backs away and protest, "My name ain't boy it's Jordan."

Towers snarls, "It's whatever I want it to be Recruit. You in my house."

Jordan with a sneer on his face responds, "If you don't get out of my face, we going to have a problem."

Towers gets on the radio, "Can I get another JSO out here this recruit is giving me some problems."

A 6'3" tall black female with black hair coming down past her shoulder that's braided up and tied back with a black scrunchy. She has on no make-up she approaches in a calm voice and asks, "So what's going on?"

Towers explains, "He tells me we're going to have a problem if I don't get out of his face."

The new JSO looks at Jordan "Is this true?"

Jordan more relaxed, "Ma'am yes ma'am."

"I'm JSO Erickson," she looks at Towers. "I got it we good."

Towers takes a deep breath, stares down Jordan then walks away.

Erickson to Jordan, "What's your name?"

"Jordan Skyy."

"Well, Recruit Skyy I will check with my supervisor to see if I can do your intake. Is that cool?"

Jordan's more relaxed she kind of reminds him of his mom, "Ma'am yes ma'am."

They walk into the empty barracks. It is a big 10,000 square feet building with four large rooms or squad bays as they are referred to. In the squad, bays are the resident's metal bunk beds and they are bolted down to the floor. There are a total of 16 bunk beds in each squad bay, under the bottom rack is a storage bin where the residents keep their items. The bathrooms have no doors on them so the JSO can watch the residents. There have been fights in bathrooms before so the doors were removed. They are located on both sides of the building. There are several cameras located on the ceiling throughout the building. Outside the squad bay is the large open area where the company forms up for headcount and free time. At the back of the building is a long white table that goes across the barracks there are six phones on the table spread out for residents to make phone calls.

JSO Erickson to Recruit Skyy orders him, "Take a seat, I got to make a phone call."

She walks across the barracks makes a phone call after 2 minutes she hangs up the phone and goes into the office and grabs some hair clippers.

Erickson comments, "I'm going to be doing a lot of talking while I cut to get through this."

Jordan nervous about the haircut asks, "Do I have to get a haircut?"

Erickson chuckles and answers, "Yep everybody who comes into the program gets one, it just easier for us, we won't have to worry about trying to make it look good and it shows everybody is treated equal no matter who they are, besides about a month before you leave we allow it to grow back."

Jordan shakes his head mournfully, "It took me 2 years to grow this."

Erickson laughs, "It's going to take me 2 minutes to cut it." She turns the clippers on.

That night Jordan is laying on the top of a bunk bed with twelve other boys he does not know. The boy underneath him asks, "What's your name bro?"

Jordan answers, without looking down, "Jordan Skyy what's yours?"

He answers, "Brewster Allen," he is a seventeen-year-old tall 6'1" skinny white kid with dirty blond facial hair, who could be mistaken for staff if you didn't know better. "How long you here for?"

Skyy sighs, "I don't know, I just got to earn 3,600 points."

Allen explains, "That's six months if you earn 20 points a day, for six months straight and you ain't doing that. What they send you here for?"

Skyy complains, "It was some bullshit weed and gun charge and the cop capped on me says I resisted arrest. What about you?"

Allen answers, "I stole some cell phones and x boxes."

"Damn how did you do that?"

"I used to work at Best Buy."

"So, when are you leaving here?"

"I got 50 days left?"

"Is it hard here?"

Allen tells it to him straight, "I'm not going to lie I didn't think I could do it when I first got here, there are a lot of rules and certain staff don't care about doing shit to set you off, but I wanted to go home so I just fake it to make it.

Skyy replies, "I'm not sure I can do that, JSO Towers is a punk ass."

Allen admits, "Yeah he is one of the main ones you need to watch out for."

Suddenly a short black JSO looks into the squad bay knocks on the window and yells, "Y'all need to be quiet in there."

Allen yells, "Sir yes sir."

He opens the squad bay door in a threatening tone states, "If you wake anybody up I'm have you come out and do extra military instruction until I get off and I got seven hours left," he shuts the door.

Skyy turns over faces away from the window and whispers, "Later."

CHAPTER THIRTY-FOUR

The squad bay door is slammed open against the wall shocking Jordan awake, the JSO standing at the door is kicking it with the heel of his boot, yelling, "Get up, Let's Go! Let's Go!"

Recruit Skyy jumps down from the top bunk puts on his shower slides and runs out of the squad bay following the other residents. Everyone is running out to the day area and standing at attention side by side.

Sgt. Crawford stands in front of the residents and yells, "Attention!"

They all yell, "Snap" in unison. Sgt. Crawford then yells, Count off!"

The residents from left to right yell, "Sir 1 sir, Sir 2 sir... counting till the last person yells, "Sir 46 sir."

Four JSO's walk through the ranks giving them toothpaste on their toothbrushes.

Sgt. Crawford then yells, "All right fall out to your designated heads to care for your personal hygiene."

The JSO's then falls outside the bathroom to monitor the residents. Recruit Skyy follows behind Cadet Allen and following his movements. They go back to their squad bay. JSO Bentley is standing outside the squad bay, He tells Recruit Skyy, "Ok I see Cadet Allen is helping you." He looks at Allen and nods, "Continue working with him making his rack and whatnot."

"Sir yes sir," Allen sounds off with.

JSO Bentley stands in the doorway watching the residents, making their beds. He asks, Recruit Skyy, "Have you made your intake phone call?"

"Sir no sir, when I called my mother she could not talk, she was at work."

Bentley replies, "We should get the chance today," looks at his watch yells, "We got five minutes.

Sr. Cadet Allen is tightening up his rack, "All right I will help you" they both start working on Jordan's bunk, if not the best but it's a start. They then start to get dressed putting on their battle dress uniform, Recruit Skyy puts on his gray recruit shirt and Cadet Allen puts on his purple Cadet shirt and their military combat boots.

Sgt. Crawford from in front of the control desk yells 10.......9.......counting down the residents start a mad scramble to finish up, Sgt. Crawford continues 5.......4.... they start to go to the day area, taking seat legs crossed left over right, right-hand right knee, left hand left knee.

3....2.......1.... All residents yell together, "Freeze Resident Freeze!"

Sgt. Crawford pacing back in forth, "Listen up today is the first day of school, so we will no longer be doing pt in the morning it will be after school sometime and on second shift. We will be going to breakfast right now and right after breakfast to school any questions?"

"Sir no sir" they all sound off together.

JSO Gilmore stands at the barracks door, yells, "Sr. Cadets on the hatch" five residents go to the door and line up 2 by 2 the rest of the company falls in the same order after everybody is lined up.

JSO Gilmore really loud, "HALF STEP." The residents yelling louder, "LEFT FOOT, Gilmore continues, "MARCH! They all march out of the barracks and down the sidewalk to the chow hall.

"Recruit Skyy I'm Mrs. Roebuck I will be your, case manager, during your time at boot camp." She is a dark-skinned black woman in her mid-40's with a short bob-layered hairstyle cut so it is laid to the left side of her face slightly covering her eye. She wears a pair of black metal semi-circle glasses. She has a very serious vibe about her.

She continues, "I am sorry about yesterday that is not normally how the intake is supposed to take place, but we have learned to adjust on the fly. So, do you have any questions about anything?"

Jordan replies, "Ma'am I was talking to someone about the points and going home, but I wasn't sure what he was saying

"Well the program is based on daily points, you have 3 opportunities to earn points throughout the day 1st $2^{nd,}$ and 3rd shift. The most you can earn per shift is 9 on 1st, 9 on $2^{nd,}$ and 2 on 3rd for a total of 20. You must earn a total of 3,600 points to graduate from this program. The math works out if you earn 20 points per day for 180 days which is 6 months you get 3,600 points. The way it is set up is you are supposed to do your 1st month as a Recruit in the gray shirt. After you get 400 points, you advance to the next phase as a Cadet which is the purple shirt. This is supposed to take four months. After that is the last phase the Senior Cadet which is the gold shirt. To become a senior cadet, you have to pass a test and all staff from JSO's, case management, any therapist you might see, teachers, and even a select few cadets decide if they think you're ready to be a senior cadet. Any questions?'

Recruit Skyy shook his head yes, asks, "So how do I earn points?"

Mrs. Roebuck, "Basically just doing the program, going to school, doing PT following staff instructions, getting along with your peers making progress in any groups that you are in. I'm not going to say it will be easy, but you can do it if you set your mind to it and want to do it."

Recruit Skyy inquires, "So what happens if I don't do the program?"

Mrs. Roebuck surprised by the question asks him in a serious tone, "Do you plan on being a problem? From reading your paperwork you should be grateful for the opportunity to be in this program, you were looking at years with your felony charges. If you act out, you will be placed in the brig, just wasting your time not earning any points towards leaving here. Hopefully, you will do the right thing and take advantage of this opportunity, there are going to be staff who test you just like there will be residents, all the staff want to see you graduate they just have a different way of doing it."

Recruit Skyy squirms in the chair, "I was just asking."

Mrs. Roebuck adds, "Now my job with you is to address any issues and concerns you might have, I will be keeping your parents and probation officer updated on how you're doing, I will be doing that by doing a case plan that we will do once every 2 weeks. If you have any school, medical or mental issues you can request to speak to me, and hopefully we can take care of them. Have you had a chance to speak to your family yet?"

"Ma'am no ma'am I was told I would today."

Mrs. Roebuck shuffles through some forms, "Ok I see I got your mother's number here would you like to call her?"

Recruit Skyy excitedly answers, "Ma'am yes ma'am."

She picks up the phone and starts dialing, "I going to transfer to the phone outside on the quarter deck."

A phone starts ringing outside her office, "The line is ringing go pick it up."

Recruit Skyy leaves her office and picks up the phone.

Vicky driving to work hits the phone button on her car, "Hello"

"Hello, mom?"

Vicky is excited to hear his voice, *"Hey Jordan how are you doing?"*

"I'm good, I'm at boot camp.

Vicky asks, *"So how is it so far?"*

Recruit Skyy says, *"They do a lot of yelling and screaming, there are a lot of rules."*

Vicky is a little nervous when she hears this, *"So how are you dealing with that?"*

Recruit Skyy takes a deep breath, *"Ok I guess, there is the one dude who is an asshole that got in my face, I think he is trying to get me in trouble."*

Vicky encourages him, *"Look stay strong son, don't let them get to you, do what you need to do before you know it you will be home."*

Jordan takes a deep breath, *"I'll try, then he whines, I don't want to be here can't you get me out?"*

Vicky exclaims *"How after what you did in court? What can I do? You just got yourself in a situation that I can't fix. Just do what you need to do to come home. We all miss you especially KJ."*

Recruit Skyy sighs, *"Yeah I miss y'all too. So, everybody is good? Have you heard from Reign?"*

Vicky replies, *"No I haven't heard from her since she last came by. We're all good you know it's the first day of school I've just been busy with that."*

Recruit Skyy's disappointed, *"So when can you come to visit."*

"I'm not sure hopefully this weekend if not then next weekend."

Mrs. Roebuck from her office yells, *"Times up."*

Recruit Skyy hears this, *"Mom I got to go."*

Vicky asks, *"So when can you call again?"*

"I don't know I think we get one call a week."

Mrs. Roebuck louder from her office, *"You need to hang up now."*

"Bye Mom, love you,"

CHAPTER THIRTY-FIVE

It's a beautiful sunny afternoon, the company is outside in the big field doing physical training. There are different stations set up with between 7-10 residents at each station with a JSO at each station monitoring the exercises, there is a track circling the field and residents are running/walking around it. Sgt. Crawford is in the center of the field with a whistle and stopwatch. Skyy is at the jumping jack station, JSO Bentley is monitoring the group he is already exhausted 15 minutes in.

Recruit Skyy stops doing the jumping jacks, sweating bending down hands on his knees asks, "How long do we have to do this?"

JSO Bentley, "You have two minutes come on don't quit keep pushing yourself."

Recruit Skyy starts back up with a poor effort, Sgt. Crawford blows the whistle yells, "Switch."

Recruit Skyy follows the group to the next station, which is pushups, he asks the Cadet beside him, "How long is PT?"

"About one hour."

Crawford blows his whistle yells, "Begin."

They all drop to the ground and start doing push-ups, 30 seconds in Recruit Skyy drops to the ground lies flat on his stomach.

JSO Erickson claps her hands, and yells, "Let's go recruit, let's go."

He pushes himself off the ground thinks, *"This shit is crazy, they trying to kill me."* He goes to his knee's girl-style pushups, holding his body up for about 10 seconds, and collapses to the ground again.

JSO Erickson bends down and looks at him face to face, "That's it? Are you done? Pitiful." She shakes her head and stands back up. Once again Crawford blows the whistle yells, "Switch."

The whole group gets up and shuffles towards JSO Towers who is on the track. Jordan walking/shuffling thinks, *Great now I got to deal with this asshole.*

Towers yells at Recruit Skyy, "Come on we can't start to you get up here." Skyy makes it to the starting point, "One mile, six laps around, let me know what lap you're on when you pass by. GO!!"

Everybody takes off. About halfway around Skyy's in the rear starts walking the track,

Towers yells across the field, "Keep running, there is no walking on my track."

Recruit Skyy walks a few more steps and then takes off with a shuffle/walk. He passes by Towers without saying anything, Towers yells at him, "You need to sound off with what lap you're on." Skyy just keeps walking/shuffling without responding.

At about the same spot as last time, he stops and starts walking. Some of the other residents are starting to lap him.

Towers yells at him, "The longer you walk the longer you're going to be out here."

Skyy thinks, *"Does he ever shut up?"*

Cadet Allen comes up behind him, "Come on bro I'll run with you."

He slows down and they both start running together, after about one hundred yards, he stops again, Allen slows down but Skyy waves him off, Allen continues running.

About 50 yards away from Towers he starts to shuffle again, he passes by him again without saying anything.

Towers shouts, "I told you to sound off when you passed me. Get over here."

Skyy continues to shuffle/walk from him.

Towers takes off after him and gets in his face, screams at him, "You need to answer me when I'm talking to you!!"

Recruit Skyy looks up at him yells back at him, "You need to get the fuck out of my face!"

Towers bumps him with his chest, "Or what?? What are you going to do??"

Recruit Skyy pushes him in the chest, Towers slips on the track. JSO Erickson sees this and runs up behind Recruit Skyy. She is attempting to restrain him, and he is resisting, Towers regains his footing and grabs his legs causing him to fall face-first on the track. Sgt. Crawford blows the whistle loud and yells, "Everybody hit the deck." All the residents stop and lay on their stomachs with their hands spread out and their palms facing up. JSO Towers has his handcuffs out and is placing them on Jordan's right wrist. JSO Bentley comes over to assist. They get Recruit Skyy handcuffed Bentley, and Erickson helps him to his feet.

Bentley offers, "I will take him to the brig." They start walking to the barracks.

In the barracks, the brigs are in the back, they are six solitary rooms with only a sink and toilet in them.

JSO Gilmore is in the barracks doing brig watch, Recruit Skyy is walked into the area and passes by the dude who got restrained from the fight. He is in the first brig.

JSO Bentley at the brig door, asks Recruit Skyy, "Were you hurt?"

"No."

JSO Bentley lets him out of the cuffs Recruit Skyy goes into the brig the heavy metal door is shut. He sits down on the concrete floor rocking back and forth, and crying mumbling over and over, "I can't do this."

CHAPTER THIRTY-SIX

The resident in the brig, next to him, comes to the door yells through the crack, "Fool what you crying for?"

Recruit Skyy, still sitting down on the floor yells back, "Shut up."

"So why you in the brig?"

"That tall racist asshole keeps messing with me."

"You talking about Towers? Yeah, he is straight-up an asshole. What's your name?"

"Jordan Skyy, What's yours?"

"Tyaramis Wilkins, they call me T Lex. What set you belong to?" He is 5'7" dark-skinned muscled up with the three dots tattoo on the right eye on the outside corner. On his right forearm is the number 169 in Kings cross font tattooed going down his arm. On the other arm is a crude clown happy/sad face mask. He is gang-affiliated and proud of it.

Skyy answers, "Set? Fool I ain't banging."

Tyaramis confides, "Well I'm starting something here. Some of these fools be trippin in here. You down?"

Recruit Skyy replies, "Whatever fool I just need to get out of here," he gets up off the floor and lies down on the cement block asks, "So how long you been here?"

Ty sits down, "Two months and I'm still a recruit, my county is going to have to pull me I'm not doing this program."

JSO Gilmore coming back their checks the residents, "Y'all need to be quiet back here if you want to be compliant."

Tyaramis yells, "Aw shut up bro."

Gilmore looks into the brig and laughs he walks to Jordan's brig, "If you want to get out you need to be compliant."

Jordan still lying down mutters, "I don't care I'm not coming out."

Gilmore shakes his head, "Suit yourself it's your life," he walks away.

Vicky's in the kitchen is on the phone with Mrs. Roebuck, "I'm would like to schedule a visit with Jordan Skyy."

Mrs. Roebuck quietly says, "I'm sorry to tell you that Jordan has been in room confinement for the last 4 days refusing to come out saying that he is not going to do the program."

Vicky disappointed to hear this sighs, "So why is he in room confinement?"

"He was disrespectful towards staff and got aggressive and had to be physically restrained and since then he has been non-compliant."

Vicky asks, "Is there anything I can do?

Mrs. Roebuck responds, "Well once we get him out the brig, we might try to let him call and talk with you to see if you can get through to him."

"No problem call me any time. Goodbye."

She walks to the kitchen table where KJ and Ericka are eating.

KJ asks, "So how is Jordan?"

"Not good he is in room confinement."

The doorbell rings and KJ gets up from the table, "I got it" he opens it, Reign is standing there.

KJ opens the door hollers, "It's Jordan's girlfriend."

Vicky gets up and walks to the living room, "Come in honey, so good to see you."

Reign comes in and sits on the couch, KJ goes back to the kitchen and Vicky sits down beside her.

Reign says, "I'm sorry for just dropping by I just finished basketball practice and was driving by I wanted to see how Jordan's doing."

Vicky wipes away a tear, "I just got off the phone, he is not doing well at all, they say he is in room confinement and will not come out."

Reign shakes her head. "I was hoping you were going to tell me everything is good. So, have you talked to him?"

"Not since he first got there, he did asks about you."

"I miss him; I wish he was doing better. She pauses. "You think I can write him a letter?"

Vicky smiles, "You know what he would like that, but he is only allowed to get letters from me, I tell you what, you write a letter and I will send it with mine, I'm writing him sometime next week."

Reign promises, "Okay I will start tonight."

Vicky suggests, "Maybe this will get him focused to do what he needs to do. So how is everything with you?"

"It's okay just been busy with school basketball and work. Well I see y'all eating so I will go just wanted to see how Jordan's doing and I don't have your number."

Vicky grabs her phone, "Here put your number in you can text me when you're coming by and I'll keep you updated."

Reign puts her number in. She stands, "Well I'm going now, and I'll stop by with the letter next week."

CHAPTER THIRTY-SEVEN

Monday morning the company is at school and JSO Erickson is monitoring the residents in the brig. Both case managers Mrs. Roebuck and Mr. Grayson come into the barracks. He is a tall 6'2" white man with a salt and pepper hair comb over he looks to be in his 40's with a potbelly. They walk over to JSO Erickson.

Mrs. Roebuck asks Erickson, "So how have they been doing?"

Erickson replies, "Well you know Recruit Wilkes is being Recruit Wilkes. He's talking a bunch of gang nonsense. Recruit Skyy is just following his lead."

Mrs. Roebuck says, "Let's go I want to talk to him and see if we can get him to come out."

Recruit Wilkes comes to the door and presses his face against the Plexiglas and yells, "The 169 boys, in the house."

JSO Erickson punches the glass, tells him, "Go sit down."

They all walk back to Recruit Skyy's brig cell. JSO Erickson opens the door. Mrs. Roebuck, steps to the front, "Come on out Skyy we would like to talk with you."

Recruit Skyy gets up and they all walk to the back counter. Erickson grabs four chairs and all four sit down in a small circle.

Mrs. Roebuck states, "You've been in there for almost a week and got 0 points, what can we do to get you to do this program?"

Jordan snaps, "You can fire Mr. Towers."

Mrs. Roebuck replies, "Come on be reasonable, if you feel like Mr. Towers has violated your rights you can file a grievance and we will look into it. Ms. Erickson can help you do that."

Recruit Skyy looks at Erickson, "I don't understand you. You were cool when you did my intake, then you flipped that day we were doing PT."

JSO Erickson looks back at him and explains, "I'm not here to be your friend, this is my job, for your intake, I was defusing a situation, but when I see you get disrespectful and aggressive towards staff I'm always going to have staff back. I can be as chill as the next person, but don't get it twisted. We are not friends, but I will help you file a grievance when you get the chance."

He is confused about what he heard and doesn't say anything.

Mrs. Roebuck continues, "I talked with your mother last week, she was very upset hearing that you weren't doing the program. Even if you don't care about yourself do it for her, I can tell she loves you and wants you home as soon as possible. So, you ready to come out and do this?"

Recruit Skyy takes a deep breath responds, "Okay."

Mrs. Roebuck, "Good! I will see you in school." She then tells Erickson "Let Wilkes out, he has been in long enough." Both Mrs. Roebuck and Mr. Grayson get up and walk out of the barracks.

Erickson stands up, "All right Recruit Skyy, get dressed, I will have to call to let them know you are coming up." Shaking her head says, "I still have Recruit Wilkes to get ready, I'll be glad when they pull that fool."

Recruit Skyy is in his English class with Mrs. High who is out of the room. He notices Joey Waddles his friend from Detention is there.

Recruit Skyy sits at the desk behind him and asks, "When you get here?"

Recruit Waddles replies, "I've been here for 3 days."

Recruit Skyy responds, "Cool, I been in the brig for about a week."

"So, I guess you don't like it here?"

"Bro, I hate it here."

Recruit Waddles shrugs, "It is what you make of it."

Mrs. High comes back into the class and following her is Recruit Wilkes, the bro from the brig he was talking with. He takes a seat to the left of Recruit Skyy.

Wilkes leans in close whispers, "You thought about what we talked about in the brig?"

Mrs. High from her desk, "You two need to be quiet."

Recruit Wilkes in a sympathetic tone replies, "Sorry Mrs. High." He whispers to Recruit Skyy, "I will get with you later."

After school, the whole company is in the barracks. Sgt. Crawford says loudly, "Ok Mr. Grayson's anger management class will be meeting in 15 minutes. Recruit Skyy you are in that group. Mr. Gilmore get everybody on the hatch."

JSO Gilmore hollers, "Okay if you are in Mr. Grayson's anger management get on the hatch."

Recruit Skyy and nine other residents including Recruit Wilkes line up on the hatch in 2 columns.

JSO Gilmore calls out, "Skyy get on the hatch." He falls out of formation and opens the door.

Gilmore yells, "Half step."

The residents reply, "Left foot, march" and they all march out the door.

In the classroom area, all nine residents are sitting at a desk, JSO Gilmore is at the back of the class waiting for Mr. Grayson.

Mr. Grayson comes to the classroom announces, "Sorry I'm late I just got caught up on the phone with a parent."

He walks to the desk, JSO Gilmore steps out of the class and shuts the door.

He looks around and notices Recruit Skyy, "I see we have a new student; can you stand up and introduce yourself."

He stands up announces, "Jordan Skyy."

Mr. Grayson stands up, "Thank you Recruit Skyy. You can take a seat. Now to tell you a little bit about the group, we are here to work on our anger. Why we get mad, what gets you mad, how we can control our anger, the main rule we follow is what is said in here stays in here just like Vegas. Just a little joke. So, Recruit Skyy why are you here with us?"

"Well, I got sent here by the judge."

Mr. Grayson replies, "We know that, why are you here?"

"Ok, I got lied on by a crooked cop."

"No, you're going to have to dig deeper than that."

"I don't understand what you're asking."

He walks up to him and says earnestly, "Look you going to have to dig deep inside to find the true reason you are here, we will get back to you."

Dejuan is at a convenience store with his boy Tristan. He walks to Tristan's car when Reign pulls into the gas pump. Both she and Zoey get out of the car, Reign hands Zoey some money and says, "Here's a 20 for pump 6."

Zoey walks to the store and turns around and asks, "Can I get something to drink?"

"Sure, take it out that 20."

Tristan goes to the car; Dejuan walks over towards Reign.

Reign is at the pump waiting for it to be turned on when she sees Dejuan walking towards her.

Dejuan asks, "Where you been? Y'all moved."

Reign retorts, "How would you know? You've been to my house?"

Dejuan probes, "So where do you live now?"

Reign hears the gas pump ping and starts putting gas in her car. "Why would I tell you that? So, you can come and harass me?"

Dejuan smirks, "So your man is locked up. How is he doing?"

Reign annoyed, "So you going there? Why are you over here? Can't you get the message, we were done, over, finished I don't answer your calls, texts, post, nothing. Why are you asking about him you don't care, I still believe you pulled a gun on him."

Zoey walks out of the store drinking a Mountain Dew soda she gets in the car.

Reign finishes pumping the gas. "Look I gotta go, move on with your life everybody will be happier."

Dejuan doesn't respond, he just watches as she drives away.

He gets into Tristan's car, "I need to find out where she lives."

Tristan asks, "How are you going to do that?

"Follow her."

"Right now?"

"No fool she's seen me. After she gets out of school, I will follow her then."

CHAPTER THIRTY-EIGHT

The company is in the gym, playing basketball Recruit Skyy is on the sidelines watching the game with his bro Recruit Waddles he asks, "So you going to start doing the program?"

Recruit Skyy admits, "I'm trying bro as long as that asshole Towers stays away from me."

Recruit Waddles advises, "You shouldn't let one person stand in the way of doing what you need to do to get out of here."

"Yeah, that's easy for you to say. He ain't messing with you."

"Don't you have a family, friends, girlfriend, that you want to get back to you?"

"Yeah bro, my girl Reign, we were feelin each other when I got arrested. Her crazy ass ex came to my job and drew down on me, I was about to get back with this fool when I got arrested."

Recruit Wilkins and another recruit come and sit down on the opposite side of Recruit Waddles.

Wilkins sits close to Skyy, "Yo this is my bro Tony," Tony is 5'8" a mixed kid half black and half Mexican he is slightly overweight not fat just his belly hangs over the waistband of his shorts, he extends out his hand and they dap out.

Recruit Wilkins whispers to Skyy, "Yo dog we thinking about getting out of here?"

Recruit Skyy asks, "What? How?"

Wilkins in a low voice, "Chill down bro. You know they have to keep the squad doors open overnight. So, when they come to do their checks, we jump them, take the keys, and shut the hatch on them."

Tony leans down and asks, "So you in or not?"

Skyy murmurs, "Bro chill y'all just dropping this on me, let me think about it."

Wilkins answers "We need to know real soon, we trying to do it Friday.

Skyy sits there and thinks to himself, *I hate this place, I shouldn't even be here, I could get back with Reign and take care of that fool DJ.*

He leans over to Wilkins and in a low voice says, "Alright I'm in."

CHAPTER THIRTY-NINE

Reign stops by Jordan's house on the way to school. She rings the doorbell and Vicky answers the door.

"Here is my letter to Jordan." she hands her one folded piece of paper.

Vicky grabs the letter assures her, "Ok I promise I won't read it," and stuffs it in her purse, "I don't have a lot of time to talk I'm dropping the kids at school then I'm off to work."

Ericka and KJ walk behind her, KJ just gives her the "What's up head bob." Ericka's right behind him, smiles, and waves at her. Reign waves back as she walks to her car.

Vicky from the car tells her, "I'm going to mail it after I get off today."

In the barracks, the company was doing free time, when Mrs. Roebuck and Mr. Grayson walk in. They go into the office to speak with Sgt. Dell. Mr. Grayson closes the door.

Mr. Grayson to Sgt. Dell, "I got this statement from Recruit Waddles, it says that Wilkins, Skyy, and Jameson are talking about breaking out of here Friday night." He hands the paper to Sgt. Dell, who reads it.

In the gym, while we're playing basketball, I heard Wilkins, Skyy, and Jameson, talking about jumping staff and breaking out of here Friday on third shift.

Recruit Waddles, Can I get some extra points?

Sgt. Dell suggests, "Well we need to call each one in here and talk with them to see if this is real. We don't need to call Waddles in here first this might tip the others off that we know something. Let's go ahead and get Wilkes first, I'm sure he is the ringleader and the one most likely to act stupid."

Sgt. Dell opens the office door and calls out, "Recruit Wilkes come here."

Wilkes looks at Jameson, gets up, and shuffles to the office, "Recruit Wilkes reporting as order sir."

Sgt. Dell says, "Come in and shut the door."

Wilkes walks in and everybody is sitting down looking at him, "Um what's going on?"

Sgt. Dell answers bluntly, "I'm get right to it, we got a report you talking about trying to escape Friday night is this true?"

Recruit Wilkes excitedly, "What!! Who told you that?"

Sgt. Dell stands up in a serious tone, "You need to calm down and you didn't answer the question."

Wilkes exclaims, "Bro, I don't know what the hell y'all talking about."

Mr. Grayson, holding up a stack of papers. "So, you're telling us that all these statements are a lie?

You've been here for 3 months and don't have any points. Why should we believe you?"

Wilkes looks at the statements unconcerned says, "I know those statements are fake because my homeys wouldn't snitch on me."

Sgt. Dell says, "Alright keep that same energy as we go to the brig until we can investigate this all the way through."

He stands up and walks towards him, "Let's go."

Wilkes angrily yells, "This is bullshit, how long I'm in here for?"

"Don't know could be a day could be a week, depends on the investigation," he replies as they stop at the brig door. "Take off your shoes and step in."

Wilkes takes off his shoes, and slams the door shut, with his back turn starts kicking the steel door with the heel of his foot yelling, "Fuck boot camp, Fuck boot camp," over and over.

Sgt. Dell walks away.

Before he goes into the office he yells, "Recruit Skyy get over here."

Recruit Skyy is sitting at a table playing a game of chess, with Allen questions, "I wonder what the hell is going on?"

He shuffles over to the office, Sgt. Dell looks at him sternly, "You need to tell us the truth."

Skyy with a confused look stammer, "What...?"

Sgt. Dell opens the door they both walk-in, Recruit Wilkins yells, "Don't tell them shit, fuck boot camp."

Sgt. Dell states, "We heard you were part of a gang, which was going to break out of here Friday night. Is this true?"

Skyy stutters, "Um I ain't in no gang."

Sgt. Dell, replies, "That's not the point. Were you trying to break out of here Friday with Wilkes?"

Wilkes yells, "They don't know shit they just trying to get you to snitch."

Mrs. Roebuck asserts, "Were not stupid. With him yelling, it's obvious something was going on. We just trying to get you to do the responsible thing and admit to it."

"No cap bro, I don't know anything about no gang or trying to escape."

Mrs. Roebuck declares, "We've got a written statement telling us everything."

"Well if you got written statements telling y'all everything, what you need me for?"

Sgt. Dell stands up, "That's it. I'm tired of your attitude. You're going to the brig. I tried to give you a chance to come clean and you throw it in our face."

Sgt. Dell walks towards Recruit Skyy, "Turn around and open the door, Recruit Skyy just stands their stares at him. Sgt. Dell stares back at him says in a lower tone and warns him, "By choice, or by force, it don't make a difference to me but you're going to the brig."

Recruit Skyy turns around and jerks open the door. They walk down the hall past the brig Wilkins is in. He is standing at the door and yells, "Yeah bro, fuck boot camp."

They go to the next brig Sgt. Dell tells Skyy, "Take off your shoes." He shuts the door, says to Recruit Skyy through the door "It's too late for him in this program, but not you, you need to think about your future."

CHAPTER FORTY

On her way to work, Vicky gives Mrs. Roebuck a call. The phone rings four times.

"Hello, Allen County Juvenile Services."

Vicky asks, "Can I speak with Mrs. Roebuck?"

The receptionist responds, "Hold please."

After about five minutes, "This is Mrs. Roebuck how may I help you?"

"I'm Mrs. Skyy, Jordan's mother, I would like to schedule a visitation to see him this weekend."

"Mrs. Skyy, I need to let you know right now he is in the brig with some other boys. They were talking about escaping from here."

Vicky, shocked by this gasp, "Are you serious?"

"Yes, ma'am. We take talk of planning to escape from this place very seriously."

"I just don't know what is going on with that boy," she sighs. She takes a deep breath and asks, "So will he be out by Saturday."

"Well, he should as long as no other incident happens."

"Okay, can you set me up for a visit on Saturday at one?"

Mrs. Roebuck at her desk, types on her computer, "I'm putting you in right now. I would like to thank you for being an active parent."

"Excuse me, what am I supposed to do? He is my son."

"I didn't mean anything negative by it. You would be astonished by how many parents believe it is our responsibility to raise their kids once they are in the program. They just wash their hands, no calls, no visitation, no letters nothing."

"Well, you don't have to worry about that from me. I may not agree with everything he does but I will never give up on him."

"That's good to hear because it is going to take all sides, the JSO's, myself, the counselors, you, and of course Jordan himself if he is going to be successful."

Vicky pulls into the hospital parking lot. "Well thank you and see you Saturday at one."

"Have a good day." They hang up.

In the barracks, Recruit's Wilkins, Skyy, and Jameson are in the brig, rapping, banging on the doors, and just being stupid. They are yelling at each other through the door cracks.

Wilkins stands at the door and yells through the crack, "Yo how long we been in here?"

Skyy yells back through the door crack, "Four, five days. I lost count bro the days are running together."

Jameson yells through the door, "Man I'm hungry what time is lunch?"

Wilkins snaps, "Bro your fat ass always hungry."

Jameson angrily responds, "Forget you fool." He starts banging on the door with his hand yells, "Let me out" over and over.

He stops banging on the door, takes his shirt off and stuffs it in the toilet, and flushes it continuously causing the toilet to overflow. Water's spilling on the floor seeping underneath the door into the hallway. He starts yelling, "Sir my toilet, is flooding."

JSO Ashley walks down the hall sees the flooding, yells, "Really? really Jameson?" He tiptoes through the water and walks to the brig door.

Jameson standing at the door shirtless says, "I used the toilet and when I flushed it, it flooded."

"So where is your shirt?" he asks. He then walks down to the end of the hall and opens a wall panel and shuts off the water. "Just for that I'm shutting off the water for everybody's room, so this won't happen again. I'm not cleaning your room up you made the mess you clean it up."

Wilkins and Skyy start yelling, "That's not fair! When we getting out of here?"

All three start kicking and hitting the door, making a lot of noise. Mr. Ashley turns and walks away, shaking his head. He goes to the maintenance closet to get a mop and bucket. Sr. Cadet Allen comes into the barracks with the lunch trays he stops at the hatch yells out, "Sir Cadet Allen reporting as ordered."

Ashley grabbing the mop and bucket, wheels it across the day area tells him, "Fall in."

Sr. Cadet Allen pushes a cart with three Styrofoam trays on it.

Ashley asks, "So when you graduate?"

"In two weeks."

Ashley remarks, "Yeah I remember when you got here you had your mindset on doing this program, glad to see you didn't veer off course. Can you mop up the floor while I pass out lunch?"

Dejuan and Tristan drive up to LBJ High, student section, they spot Reign's red Camaro parked by the gym.

Tristan parks about fifty yards away, behind her between two other cars. Tristan asks, "So what's the plan?"

Dejuan looks at, Tristan from the passenger seat. "We just sit here until she comes out of basketball practice."

Tristan asks, "So yo dog what's up with you going 'Stan' over her?"

'Stan'?? Bro what the fuck you talking about I just love her, and she needs to see that. If she would just give me another chance. He can't love her like me. We were together for almost six months, I treated her like a queen."

"So, what is up with her man, he ain't at the Burger House no more."

"He got arrested. That night we showed up I heard he was coming after us."

"Coming after us? And do what?"

"Fool I don't know I ain't worried about that. That's old news. He's locked up."

"He's locked up and she still doesn't want to be with you? Ain't that telling you something? You looking, thirsty bro."

"Fool, I don't care what you or anybody says, we are going to be together again now shut up and watch out for her." He puts on his headphone closes his eyes and leans on the passenger side window.

Reign comes out of the gym with four other girls laughing and joking. They're all carrying white gym shoulder bags. They all hug each other, the other three girls go to a white Ford Escape, Reign continues to her car

Tristan taps Dejuan on his left shoulder his eyes are closed. "Heads up."

Dejuan sits up takes his headphones off. "Bet."

Reign puts the bag in the car and jumps in. She starts it up and takes off.

Tristan starts his car mutters, "This some crazy shit you got me doing bro."

Dejuan cautions, "Don't get too close, I don't want her to know we're here."

"I just hope she just goes straight home; I don't have a lot of gas to follow her all over the place."

"I got you."

"Yeah, just like last time, right?"

Dejuan comments, "I'm glad it's getting dark, maybe she won't notice us following. Yo fall back I know she got to be almost home. Don't want to blow it now."

Tristan responds, "Chill bro, just like she can't see us I can't see her."

She turns into the driveway and parks behind a gray Mercedes.

Dejuan yells, "Stop! Let her get out and go in the house."

They stop four houses away and watch as she parks her car in the driveway. She goes into the house.

Dejuan tells him, "Go bro, and stop in front of the house."

Tristan drives to the front of the house. Dejuan gets out of the car and takes a picture of the house and the mailbox. He gets back in the car.

"So, you not going to go up and meet the family?" Tristan jokes.

"Shut up fool, let's go."

CHAPTER FORTY-ONE

It's eight-thirty in the morning the company has just left for school. Mr. Grayson, Mrs. Roebuck, and a sheriff's deputy walk into the barracks JSO Bentley is watching the same three residents in the brig.

They walk over to Bentley. Mr. Grayson tells him, "Get some shorts and a t-shirt for Wilkes, he is getting pulled today."

Mr. Bentley is very excited to hear this and walks to the laundry room, thinks, *Cool about time! They should have pulled him a month ago.*

He gets the clothing items, and everybody walks back to the brig. Recruit Wilkins is sleeping with his back toward the door. His empty breakfast tray sits on the sink.

Bentley walks into the brig and shakes Wilkes on his shoulder he yells, "Get up, time to go."

He turns over groggily and asks, "What's going on?"

Bentley drops the clothes on top of him and informs him, "It's your lucky day. Your county is here to pick you up. Get dressed! You got five minutes."

They all step away, to give him the chance to get dressed.

After ten minutes, Bentley comes back to the brig area opens the door again. "Alright let's go you got people waiting on you."

Wilkes walks out confidently and yells, "Cool bro, finally getting the hell up out of here. 'Bout time."

The deputy pulls out some cuffs, tells him, "Place your hands in front of you." He immediately places Wilkes in handcuffs.

Mr. Grayson tells Bentley, "Go into the squad bay and get his personal items."

Bentley goes to the squad bay and grabs a folder of papers and some old blue and white Under Armor running shoes.

Bentley asks, "These your sneakers?"

Wilkes arrogantly replies, "Yeah bro, now put on me."

Bentley drops them on the ground sarcastically says, "Yeah, whatever bro." He shoves the folder and papers into his chest.

Wilkes steps into his shoes. The deputy states, "Well if that's everything we need to be going we got a three-hour trip ahead."

They all start walking, Wilkes yells out loud, "One six-nine boys out of here, later bros."

Mr. Grayson tells Bentley, "Let the other two out. The ringleader is gone."

Bentley exclaims, "Good this got old watching these fools all this time."

He goes to the laundry room and gets some uniforms for both.

He opens the door for Skyy and throws the clothes in, "Let's go your out."

He goes to Jameson's room opens the door yells, "Let's go your out."

Jameson sitting down on the floor head down says, "Sir I want to kill myself."

Bentley sighs, "So I need to put you on suicide watch?"

Jameson still sitting on the floor in a low voice replies, "Sir yes sir."

"Okay get dress so we can get to school, and I can tell your case manager. Do you have some kind of plan on how you want to do it?"

Jameson stands up puts on his pants he answers. "Sir no sir, being in this room puts some ideas in my head."

Bentley not wanting to get into any details says, "Okay you can talk about it with your case manager when we get to school."

All three of them are walking to the school when Recruit Skyy asks, "Sir, what happened with Wilkes?"

Bentley explains, "His County got tired of him wasting their time and money here, so they pulled him. He's going back to court again. I can tell you he's not going home after all the dumb stuff he did here and his original charges, there's no chance."

In the schoolhouse, JSO Bentley tells Recruit Skyy to go to school and has Recruit Jameson stand outside Mr. Grayson's office he talks with him for five minutes about Recruit Jameson's suicide comment. He leaves and Recruit Jameson goes into the office.

Mr. Grayson to Jameson, "Have a seat."

Jameson sits down in front of Mr. Grayson. Mr. Grayson asks, "So tell me what's going on?"

Recruit Jameson looking down quietly answers, "I want to kill myself."

"Why do you want to do that?"

Jameson answers, "I'm sad and depressed I miss home."

Mr. Grayson inquires, "So do you have a plan on how you want to do it?"

Jameson head still down answers, "No not really I thought about strangling myself with my bed sheet or OD' ing on some of my meds."

Mr. Grayson taking notes as he is talking takes a deep breath says, "I'm placing you on moderate watch immediately and making an appointment with the grief counselor for tomorrow, I will let you know what time later."

He gives a paper to Jameson says "Give this to Mr. Bentley you can go to school."

JSO Bentley is standing outside the office and Jameson gives him the form, he tells Jameson, "Go to class."

Mr. Grayson talks with Bentley tells him that he is placing Recruit Jameson on moderate suicide watch which means he will be placed in a white t-shirt and must be visually monitored by a JSO. All activities must be kept on a written log not to exceed 30-minute intervals. Most of the JSO's hate this because they have enough things to deal with already, and now this is an extra burden. Most JSO's know the residents use the threat of suicide as a way to get extra attention from staff, but every instance has to be treated seriously.

After school in the barracks, the company is relaxed some of them are watching TV some doing homework, playing cards, checkers, and chess. The JSO's are spread out among the residents overseeing everything.

Sgt. Dell is handing out mail to the residents.

He yells out, "Skyy you got mail."

Recruit Skyy is playing chess with Sr. Cadet Allen, he is surprised, he gets up from the table and sprints up to the desk.

Sgt. Dell looks at the envelope, "It's good to see you out the brig. Were you expecting any mail?"

"It's probably from my mom."

Sgt. Dell reads the envelope, "Yep that's who it's from, sign here." He holds out a big binder and points at a line. He then gives him the letter.

Skyy grabs the letter and runs back to the table, with Sr. Cadet Allen. He eagerly opens the letter. "It's from my mom." He unfolds three pages in his mom's handwriting.

The fourth page is written with purple ink, he looks at it and realizes it's from Reign, excited, he looks at Allen, "Yo bro my girl wrote me."

Allen quietly says, "Chill bro, you don't want to get it taken up."

He shakes his head in agreement.

He reads the letter to himself,

Jordan,

What's up boo? First, I want to say that I miss you and can't wait to see you again. I went to your house and your mom told me that you are not doing too good there. I was really sad and disappointed to hear this, I know you can do it just stay focused and do it for me. Everything is pretty good with me I don't know if you remembered but we moved about a week after you got arrested, now I live down the street we neighbors (smile). Right now, I'm pretty busy with school and basketball so I don't have a lot of time. When I went by your house to see how you were doing and talking with your mom I could tell she is really worried about you. You need to do what you have to do so you can come home, cause me and your mom both miss you and I can't wait for us to be together again. Well gotta go just wanted to drop you some lines to let you know I'm still thinking about you and can't wait to see you. Try to write back when you get the chance.*

Love Reign.

Jordan puts the letter down and smiles, "Damn bro, it's good hearing from her."

Allen prods, "Yeah bro, so what she say?"

Jordan replies, "Not much just letting me know she is thinking about me and can't wait till I come home."

Allen says, "Sounds like yo girl is ride or die."

Skyy agrees, "I know, I need to get outta here bro."

Allen states, "You know what you need to do, just gone ahead do this program."

Skyy just looks down at the letter and doesn't say anything.

Vicky wakes up Saturday morning and from her bed, she texts Reign: *I hope I'm not bothering, but I was asking if you could watch my kids, I have an appointment to see Jordan today at 1.*

Reign texts back: *I can. For how long?*

Vicky: *I should be gone for about an hour, you can come by the house and watch them here. Can you be here by 1230?*

Reign texts: *np.*

Vicky then gets on the phone and calls the Allen County Detention. After three rings it is answered

"Hello, I'm Vicky Skyy and I have an appointment today to visit my son, Jordan at one, I just wanted to check to make sure everything is still on."

"I'm Mrs. Kirkland. I will be doing the visitations today. Let me put you on hold, and I will call down to check." Three minutes later, she comes back on the line, "Yes, he is in the program."

Vicky excitedly replies, "Good don't tell him I want to surprise him."

Mrs. Kirkland says, "I won't, I'll see you this afternoon." She hangs up.

Reign and Zoey are at the front door of Jordan's house. Vicky sits anxiously on the couch. Reign rings the doorbell and Vicky jumps to answer the door. Ericka runs to the living room. Vicky looks at the time on her phone, "Thanks for being on time."

Ericka grabs Zoey's hand, "Come on let's go to my room."

They run off to play. Vicky tells Reign "Thanks for coming through on such short notice,"

Reign smiles. "It's all good, when you see Jordan tell him I said be good and I miss him."

Vicky opens the door, "I will. If anything happens call me."

Vicky pulls into the parking lot of the Allen County Juvenile Bootcamp. She walks into the building and sees an older Hispanic couple is waiting in the foyer to get into the building.

As the three of them are waiting, Vicky asks the couple, "This is my first time, is this normal?"

The man answers, "Sometimes, it' takes ten to fifteen minutes depending on how many visits' there are." Just as he is finished speaking Mrs. Kirkland comes and uses her ID badge to open the magnetic doors. Everybody walks in and she shuts the door, pushing on it to check that's it's locked.

Mrs. Kirkland is a white lady with a short blond pixie haircut, around 5'5" she's in her 30's and has on a pair of black square-rimmed glasses. She is slim, she's wearing jeans and a blue t-shirt with the words PROVE IT written in white. She sees Vicky and asks, "You're Recruit Skyy's mom? You called this morning, right?

Vicky replies, "Yes, this is my first time."

Mrs. Kirkland walks behind a counter grabs two papers, "Can I have you read the visitation rules, while I get their visitation going."

Vicky grabs the papers, "Okay."

Mrs. Kirkland gets on the phone and calls the barracks. "Can you have Cadet Hernandez report up for visitation?

Vicky is finishing up the rules when Mrs. Kirkland tells the other couple, "He should be here in a few minutes. You can have a seat in that room." She points to the room directly behind them, and they walk into the room and sit down.

Mrs. Kirkland informs Vicky, "I need the papers back and your drivers' license and your purse. You are not allowed your cell phone and you cannot give the resident anything while you are visiting with him."

Vicky reaches into her purse and gives Mrs. Kirkland her license.

Mrs. Kirkland takes it and looks at it then asks, "Can I get your purse?"

Mrs. Kirkland takes both items, "Is your phone in here?"

"Yes."

Mrs. Kirkland says, "You can go to the room on your right. If there are no questions, I will call and get Recruit Skyy."

CHAPTER FORTY-TWO

Recruit Skyy is in the barracks watching TV sitting beside Cadet Waddles. The phone rings JSO Towers answers the phone, hangs it up, and yells, "Skyy get up here."

Recruit Skyy looks at Waddle's sighs and says, "What is it now?" He remembers the last time he was called to the control desk; he shuffles up answers, "Sir Recruit Skyy reporting as ordered."

In a calmer voice, Mr. Towers says, "You have a visitation up top."

Recruit Sky breathes a sigh of relief. "I thought I was in trouble again."

JSO Towers smiles at him and replies, "Yeah, I know. I was messing with you, now get out of here."

He runs to the school enters the building yells out, "Recruit Skyy reporting as ordered."

Mrs. Kirkland yells back, "Come on."

Recruit Skyy shuffles to the other side sees his mom, tears start to well up in his eyes as he runs up to her and gives her a big hug.

She hugs him back, and he whispers, "I love you, I miss you so much."

She whispers back, "I love you too, I'm just so glad I finally get a chance to see my son."

They both sit down facing each other, and he holds her hands on his lap. He says, "It is so good to see you."

Vicky is taken back; she has never seen him so vulnerable before.

Vicky replies, "Thank you I'm just glad you are finally out so I could come visit."

Recruit Skyy moans, "Mom this place is worse than prison."

Vicky responds, "Come on Jordan you're exaggerating, it can't be that bad."

He shakes his head, "Yes, it is. All they do is yell at us all day, make us do PT every day sometimes twice a day."

Vicky suggests, "Sounds to me like they trying to teach you some respect and get you in shape."

Jordan frustrated whines, "I knew you would take their side."

Vicky states, "I'm not taken sides, I just want you to do what you have to come home."

Recruit Skyy changes the subject, "I got yours and Reign's letter yesterday. Thanks for mailing it for her. So, have you seen her lately?"

Vicky grins, "She is at the house watching KJ and Ericka." She looks directly at him and says, "I don't know what she sees in you but you need to hold on to her, I can tell she really cares for you, but you keep on acting a fool in here and she is not going to be around for long. She is a very pretty girl with a lot going on and she doesn't need no man holding her back."

Recruit Skyy lets out a big sigh, "I didn't even know if she would stick around, I thought she would move on until I got the letter. That was my best day since I been here."

Vicky asks, "So what is so difficult about this program?"

He answers, "There is this one racist JSO who is always messing with me."

Vicky shakes her head no, "Stop right there! There is always going, to be somebody who is picking on you. You said that about the cop who arrested you, now you're saying it about the staff here. You going to have to stop playin the race card every time something doesn't go your way. In life it is not always about race, the race card is a fallback excuse for weak people to cover for their faults."

Jordan is exasperated, "But mom everybody here says he racist."

Vicky explains "I don't know if he is racist or not so it's not about that. I just know, but you're going to encounter them throughout your life. You just can't let that stop you from doing what you need to do because, if it does then they win."

Jordan replies, "I know it's just so hard, getting yelled at all the time, having to wear the same clothes every day, I've been here a month and it feels like three.

Mrs. Kirkland sticks her head in the room and informs them, "You got five minutes left."

Jordan looks up at her, "Ma'am yes ma'am. So how are KJ and Ericka?"

Vicky replies, "They're both good, KJ misses you. Next time I come I will see if I can bring him. She stands up, "Well I'm get going I told Reign I'd be home in an hour."

"Thanks for coming to see me," he hugs her, she hugs him back and whispers to him, "You're welcome now you need to do your part and be good so you can come home."

He looks her in the eyes shakes his head in agreement, "Tell Reign I miss her, and thanks for writing and I love her."

Vicky looks at him and asks, "Have you ever told her this before?"

He answers, "Um no, why?"

"First, I don't believe she needs to hear it from me, and second are you really in love? Or is it this situation making you think you love her?

Jordan's head down mumbles, "I don't know maybe."

"I'll just tell her, 'you miss her' to give you time to think about your real feelings. How bout that?"

He walks out of the room and turns back says, "Cool see you next week."

CHAPTER FORTY-THREE

When Vicky pulls into the driveway, Ericka runs up to the door and opens it, "Hey mom!" Reign and Zoey are sitting on the couch she goes and takes a seat. KJ hears the commotion and comes in and sits on the floor.

Ericka excited, "So how is Jordan?"

Vicky, "Well he looks a lot different with a bald head."

KJ excited, "What? He's bald?"

Vicky, "Yeah they cut off all his hair."

KJ laughs and shakes his head.

Vicky replies, "That's not important, he's having a rough time, he was so happy to see me that he started crying."

Ericka was surprised, "Really?"

"Yeah, it was hard seeing him like that and knowing I couldn't do anything about it."

Vicky looks at Reign, "He said getting the letter from you was his best day there and that he misses you."

Reign smiles, "So do you think he will do better?"

"I don't know I had a real serious talk about doing the program so he can come home, we will see if he listened."

Reign replies, "Well at least you got a chance to see and talk to him."

Vicky inquires, "Can you keep writing him? That seemed to make him happy."

"I can do that, well" she stands up, "I got to get going."

Vicky asks, "Do I owe you anything?"

Reign walks to the door and shakes her head, "No I'm good, it gave Zoey somebody to hang with for a few hours and I wasn't doing anything."

Zoey tells Ericka, "Call me girl maybe we can get together and watch some Tik-Tok's later."

Ericka happily answers," Okay."

Vicky tells Reign, "Thanks again, okay maybe I can treat you to dinner one night."

Reign comments, "Okay you got a deal."

"Company POA move!" JSO Erickson yells.

"Snap!" they yell back, and everybody immediately comes to the position of attention.

"All right we are getting ready for Sr. Cadet Allen's graduation in fifteen minutes, Sr. Cadets get on the hatch." The four of them get on the hatch in two columns. She continues, "Cadets get on the hatch," they fall in behind the senior cadets, "Recruits get on the hatch," all twelve of them line up.

Recruit Skyy is besides Recruit Jameson, who just got released from suicide watch.

JSO Erickson loudly, "All right everybody straighten your uniform, tuck in your shirt and make sure your shoes are tied."

Recruit Skyy calls, "Ma'am Recruit Skyy request permission to speak?"

"What you need?"

"Ma'am I've never been to a graduation I don't know what to do."

Erickson walks over to him, "Just do what the person in front of you does and sound off. All right let's go, yells, "Half step... they yell back, "Left foot... March."

The company marches out the door, sounding off with "Here we go again...

In the gym, there are about 25 people in the audience, mostly staff, the JSO's, Case management, Juvenile probation officers, and schoolteachers. Sr. Cadet Allen's mom and dad are smiling in the front row.

The company marches into the gym calling cadence, "We are boot camp and we like to graduate...

After everyone has marched into the gym, JSO Erickson calls out, "Company halt." They stop, yell out, "Step place."

Sgt. Crawford steps in front of the company and faces the audience, "I would like to thank everybody for coming to Sr. Cadet Allen's graduation today, and he's asked me to give him away today. Sr. Cadet Allen is a resident who came into this program with his head on and knew he wanted to do this program. If I'm not mistaking, he hasn't been to the brig since he's been here right?" He looks at Allen, who shakes his head no. "Okay so here is Sr. Cadet Allen. He'd like to say a few words."

Sr. Cadet Allen, "Thank you for coming to my graduation...

Recruit Skyy is standing at the position of attention and he starts daydreaming. *I can't believe he's going home.* He looks out at the crowd and sees Allen's mom crying continues thinking, *Man if I was to graduate, I bet my mom would be crying just like that, I know she would be so happy. He said he faked it to make it, maybe I should do that too, I could get back with Reign. It's bullshit anyway that I'm here and Nick's home.*

JSO Erickson loudly yells, "Company POA, Move." That snaps him out of his thoughts.

"Present arms, the company salutes Sr. Cadet Allen. Allen returns the salute. Erickson yells, "Order Arms," they drop the salute.

Erickson loudly, "Half step March...

As they march out, the gym, Sgt. Crawford tells JSO Erickson, "We got school today so take us to the schoolhouse."

Recruit Skyy marching thinks, *If Allen fooled them, I should be able to. I just want to get back with Reign. Maybe I can graduate.*

The company arrives in the school area, Mrs. Roebuck calls out from her office, "Recruit Skyy fall and report to my office."

Recruit Skyy loudly replies, "Ma'am yes ma'am."

He steps out of formation and shuffles over to her office, He knocks on the door frame, "Recruit Skyy reporting as ordered."

Mrs. Roebuck sits at her desk, "Come in."

Mrs. Roebuck closes the laptop. "I'm here to do our monthly case plan, you've been in and out of the brig since you've been here so often, I wanted to take advantage of this chance while you're still out. To start with you've been here for 55 days with the chance to earn 1,100 points and you presently have 80, this is due mostly to being in the brig and earning no points and just low points for various sanction violations. Any questions?"

Recruit Skyy, sits there quietly, and shakes his head no.

"I see you got a visit from your mother. So how did that go?"

Recruit Skyy sits up in the chair excited, "It was great it was my first time seeing her since I've been here."

"That's good to hear, I've talked with your mother a few times by phone. You are a lucky young man; she loves and cares for you. Not every resident in this program has that. She is frustrated by how you are doing this program."

Recruit Skyy less excited, "True, we talked about it, I told her I was going to try and do better."

She encourages, "It's not about trying it's about being better." So how long you been out the brig?"

"About a week now."

"I'll make you a deal if you stay out for the rest of this week, I will give you an extra 140 points."

"Are you serious?"

"Yes, I'm just trying to motivate you and show you that we want you to succeed and if you put forth the effort, we will work with you."

Recruit Skyy excited, "You got a deal!"

"So last time we talked, you had some issues with JSO Towers. So how has that been going?"

"Cool, I still don't like or trust him, but I haven't had any problems with him. He was messing with me when my mom visited but is it was cool."

"That's good one last thing, you have to complete Mr. Grayson's anger management class before you can graduate, you kinda lucked out he has been ill for about the last three weeks so you haven't missed too many classes. He is back and he is having a class today after school."

Recruit Skyy, shrugs his shoulder, "Okay."

Mrs. Roebuck stands up, "If there is nothing else you can get to school."

He stands up says to her, "Don't forget our deal."

Mrs. Roebuck promises, "If you hold up your end I will mines."

After school, the company is in the barracks. Some of them are changing over to do physical training.

Sgt. Crawford to JSO Towers, "Get Mr. Grayson's anger management class on the hatch."

JSO Gilmore walks over to Towers and gives him Recruit Jameson's suicide paperwork.

JSO Towers loudly yells, "Mr. Grayson's group get on the hatch."

Twelve residents line up in a column of twos on the hatch. Recruit Skyy is in the back of the formation beside Recruit Jameson who is back in a white t-shirt on Moderate suicide watch.

Recruit Skyy whispers to Jameson, "Bro I hope he doesn't mess with me."

Towers hear them talking but doesn't know what they said and yells "Push," to both, they fall out of formation and start doing pushups.

Towers walks to the door, "Recover on your own, we need to get up to the group."

Recruit Skyy does his fifteen pushups, with perfect form, and gets back in formation, he notices a definite difference in his pushups from when he first got here.

Jameson's flopping around on the deck. Towers walks up to him and squats down shakes his head,

"That's pitiful he's been here for a month and that's the best you can do. Recover we got to go."

Jameson lying on the floor gets up and falls in formation.

Skyy looks at him and thinks, *Maybe this place is helping me.*

They march into the school building, where Mr. Grayson is already in the classroom with the desk cleared out, and the chairs set up in a circle.

After everybody's seated, Mr. Grayson says to the group, "Good afternoon it is so good to be back, as some of you might know I have been out sick for the past month but now I'm back and we have a lot of catching up to do."

He looks around the group, "I see we have some new recruits, what I like to do is have the new residents stand up introduce themselves, and tell us why they're here."

One recruit stands up, "Yo I'm Recruit Casio and I've been here for 2 weeks, and I'm here because I got snitched on."

Mr. Grayson waves his hand down motioning for him to sit down, says to him dismissively, "Ok I can see you got some things to work on."

He points at Recruit Skyy, "Your next."

Recruit Skyy stands up, "I'm not new, I guess I was in your last group before you got sick. I have been here almost 2 months and the reason I'm here is that I was a knucklehead who didn't listen to my mom and got caught up running the streets."

Mr. Grayson comments, "That's a pretty real assessment coming from a Recruit. Do you believe your anger contributed to you being here?"

Recruit Skyy shakes his head yes, "I was out of control, smoking drinking, hanging with my bros, then I got arrested and caught a resisting arrest charge which I still think is bs. In court I let my anger get the best of me and that got me here when I probably could have got probation. I have had a lot of time to think since I been here. Who knows maybe it was a good thing, I got sent here cause I needed to slow down even though, I still hate this place."

The other residents laugh.

Mr. Grayson does a golf clap, "Thank you Recruit Skyy, the first step in correcting a problem is admitting you have one, it appears you are on the right track. You can take a seat." He points to Recruit Jameson.

Recruit Jameson stands up, "What up Recruit Jameson, I've been here about a month, I am here for a family violence charge."

Mr. Grayson, "You care to explain? Everything discussed here stays with the group."

Recruit Jameson getting emotional gulps hard, "Well my mom got in my face about helping to clean up the house, she was mopping the kitchen as I was trying to get by her and she accidentally slipped on the floor and fell and broke her arm."

Mr. Grayson looks at him seriously and asks, "Are you sure it was an accident?"

Jameson's tone changes, "So what you sayin? I pushed her on purpose?"

"From the tone, you're giving me I can see that you have some anger problems."

Recruit Jameson stands up and takes an aggressive stance, "Look, bro, you don't know me so don't judge me, only GOD can judge me."

Mr. Grayson stands up and calls out, "Mr. Towers can you step in here?"

Towers walks into the classroom asks, "Is everything all right in here?"

Mr. Grayson points at Jameson, "I need this recruit removed from the class for group disruption."

Towers ask, "Does he need to go to the brig?"

Grayson thinks and shakes his head no, "Just have him do EMI (extra military instruction) until the end of class."

Recruit Jameson, pushes a chair down, and yells, "You got me fucked up I'll just go to the brig."

JSO Towers keeps his cool about Jameson knocking down the chair. He just looks at it then looks at him, "I can overlook that, there are only fifteen minutes left in class."

"I don't give a shit; I'm not doing no emi."

JSO Towers walks behind him raises his voice, "If that's the way you feel, don't talk about it, be about it. Let's go." He tells Mr. Grayson, "I will have another JSO come up to watch these residents." As they are walking out of the class, Recruit Jameson says in an angry tone "I will kill myself." JSO Towers in a frustrated tone, "You are already on Mod watch. Do we need to place you on high suicide watch?"

Recruit Jameson doesn't answer.

After they leave, Mr. Grayson sits back down, "Well that's an example of your emotions controlling you instead of you controlling your emotions. I don't have a lot of time left. Your assignment for the next group is to think of five things that get you angry and what you could do instead of getting angry."

JSO Gilmore walks into the classroom asks, "Is everything good?"

Mr. Grayson takes a deep breath, "Yeah, I'm still recovering, we're going to end early. Can you take them down to the barracks?"

JSO Gilmore, "No problem SPOA move...

CHAPTER FORTY-FOUR

LBJ High girls' varsity is playing their main rival Bryant High. Both teams are huddled on the sidelines during a time-out. There are six seconds left on the clock, the score is 69-67 LBJ is down. The whistle blows and both teams break from their huddle and walk to the court. LBJ takes the ball out on their side of the court. Reign and Chloe both walk on the court for LBJ. The LBJ forward is passing the ball in, Reign is at the top of the key, and Chloe goes to the corner baseline. The Bryant guard is playing man-to-man defense. When the referee blows the whistle, the forward slaps the ball with her right hand and Reign runs from the top of the key to the sideline where she is passed the ball. She dribbles to the top of the key, the Bryant guard crouches down and slaps the floor, the forward runs down to the baseline while Chloe runs to the top of the key to set a screen. She sets the screen to the left for Reign, Reign does a crossover dribble and drives left to use the screen. The Bryant player switches, Reign drives just inside the lane stops for the pull-up jumper. The Bryant player jumps with her and hits her hand, the ball hits the front of the rim and falls away. The referee blows the whistle and calls the foul. Reign walks to the free-throw line when her coach gets up and calls a timeout. Both teams hustle to the sidelines. Reign's coach tells her, "I wanted to call the timeout before they did to ice you. Listen this is no big deal. You've shot thousands of free throws, just breathe, relax and shoot just like you are in the gym by yourself." He tells the rest of the team, "It's a one for one, so if she misses, I need everybody to crash the board, maybe we can get a miracle put back."

The official blows the whistle, both teams are back on court lining for the free throws. Reign steps to the free-throw line takes three deep breaths and bounces the ball three times. She thinks *like coach said I've done this a thousand times*. Shoots the ball, "Swish." The crowd jumps to their feet cheering, the referee gets the ball and passes it back to her, the crowd settles down. Reign thinks, *Okay same thing*. She takes three deep breaths, dribbles three-time, shoots, the ball spins in and out of the rim. The Bryant player underneath the basket taps the ball to the backcourt over Reign's head as the buzzer goes off. The Bryant players run off jumping and high-fiving each other. Reign squats down at the free-throw line, head down looking at the floor. Chloe and the rest of the team walk over to console her.

Tristan and Dejuan are at the game both stand up. Tristan looks at Dejuan complains, "She choked! All she had to do was hit the free throw and we'd be in overtime,"

Dejuan snaps back, "Shut fool like you could have done better."

Tristan comes back with, "Fool you been on the court with me, you know what's up."

Dejuan stares at Reign as she walks off the court.

Tristan urges, "Alright let's bounce."

"Hold up bro, maybe I can talk with her you know comfort her."

"Are you serious bro? I just came to watch the game. You do you." He walks always.

Dejuan stands there and watches as Reign and Chloe walk off the court.

Reign and Chloe walk out of the locker room, both are carrying their white gym bags.

Reign is still down about the loss, "I can't believe I missed it. We lost because of me."

Chloe stops and grabs her by the arm. "Is that what you think? The only reason it was close is because of you. Did you see your stats? Twenty-four points, nine assists, seven boards, you had a hell of a game."

Reign smiles at her says, "Thanks, but I missed the one that counted."

They continue walking, "We play'em again in two weeks in their house. We'll get it back."

"You're right, I just have to hear about it, I still got a lot of friends there. I know they gonna be trolling me on Instagram."

"Girl don't even sweat that. Can you give me a ride home?"

"I got you. Do you want to study together for the chemistry test tomorrow at my house?"

"Okay let me text my mom to let her know what's up." She stops and opens her gym bag and looks through it, "Damn I can't find my phone. Can you call it?"

"Sure." She pulls her phone out of her jacket pocket and calls it says, "It's ringing."

Chloe moans, "I don't hear it, maybe I left it in the locker room." She turns around and heads back to the locker room

Reign asks, "You want me to come?"

Chloe hollers back, "No go ahead I will meet you at your car."

Reign walks out of the gym to the parking lot there are quite a few cars still there, as she gets closer to her car, she sees Dejuan with his back turned leaning on the trunk of her car.

Reign surprised to see him asks, "What are you doing on my car?"

Dejuan turns around. "I was at the game and I saw what happened, I just thought you might want someone to talk to."

Reign is surprised by his compassion. "Thanks, but I'm good."

He walks towards her. "I just want you to know that I'm here for you." He stops at the back window of the car. When she turns and faces him, he grabs her hand.

She snatches her hand away, "Look I appreciate you, but like I keep telling you we're done, I'm with Jordan, and I'm down for him."

"Why you bring him up he ain't even around."

"Just because he ain't here don't mean I'm a mess around on him."

He grabs her hand again squeezes it hard and pulls her into his body, "So what's he got that I ain't? Why you so stuck on him?"

Reign jerks her hand away and pushes away from him, "You're hurting me. Let go of me."

Chloe runs up, pulls Reign further away from Dejuan, and gets in between them "What the fuck is going on!"

DJ slowly backs away. "We were just talking."

Chloe says to DJ, "It looked like more than talking to me." Looks at Reign, "You good girl?"

Reign a little shaken up answers, "Yeah I'm okay."

Chloe looks at DJ yells, "You need to leave. NOW!"

DJ looks at Reign, "Actually I came to asks can I get a ride? My boy left me."

They both start yelling over each other, "Are you stupid? Get the hell out of here, you got some balls after what you just did."

He slowly backs away from the car, Reign clicks open the car doors, yells at him, "Next time I see you I'm calling the cops, you crazy." Both she and Chloe get in the car and drive off.

Dejuan stands there for a minute watches Reign drive away. Says to himself, *I guess I'll check out the boys' game maybe I can catch a ride from somebody in there.* He starts walking back to the gym, angry at how that played out thinks, *"Damn, that nigga locked up and I still can't with her. I don't know what to do.*

CHAPTER FORTY-FIVE

Dear Jordan,

What's up Boo, I'm sorry I haven't written in a minute. I don't have a lot of time, just wanted to write to let you know I'm still thinking about you. I've been so busy with school and basketball just haven't had time to catch my breath. I've talked with your mom she told me that you doing a lot better. I am so happy to hear that, I can't wait for us to be together again. So, do you know when you are getting out? I'm tell you something because I want to be honest with you. DJ has still been trying to get with me. He showed up at the game three weeks ago and he was at my car after the game. He grabbed me, my girl, Chloe came, and we chased him off. I haven't seen or heard from him since then. He believes since you're not around that he has a chance. I keep telling him that we are done, hopefully, he will finally get the message. Please do not let this mess up how you are doing, I just wanted to tell you what's up. Well, that's all for right now, got early practice in the morning. Check out the picture.

Keep doing good.

Love Reign Sparks.

Jordan excitedly looks inside the envelope and finds a picture of Reign in the gym wearing her home white LBJ basketball uniform. On the front is LBJ and 21 in maroon, it has a maroon thin stripe running down the side. She is posing with a basketball under her right arm. He pulls the picture out and checks it out.

With a big smile he says, Bro check out the picture." He hands it to Cadet Waddles, who looks at his head and shakes his head approvingly.

"Damn bro she fire I knew you talked about her, but I didn't think you could do this good. Bro I would do whatever I needed to do to get back to her. I know some fools out there trying to get with her."

Recruit Kareem Workman is Waddle's boy from back in their hood he's sitting down beside them. He is a dark-skinned brother about 6'0" about 175 pounds pretty muscular. He plays both football and basketball in school. He is chill for the most part but does have a temper when pushed. He is reading a book, puts it down says, "Let me see." He takes the picture and smiles, "No cap, I would take my shot."

Cadet Skyy snatches the picture back, "Shut up fool she told me, Dejuan her ex is still pushing up on her."

"I guess with you not around that nigga's taken another shot."

Cadet Skyy just sits there, imagining Dejuan messing with Reign, then he drifts back wondering about the night DJ pulled the gun on him. *Should I have done something differently?*

Cadet Waddles messes with Skyy, "You don't think they smashed up do you?"

Cadet Skyy hears the question and shakes his head back to reality. "Bro shut the hell up she wouldn't even tell me about it if she got back with him."

Waddles grins, "Yeah I guess you're right." He looks at the chessboard, "Come on let's finish the game."

JSO Ashley calls out to Waddles, "Who are you calling?"

"I'm calling my grandmother." He gets ups and walks to the back of the barracks there is a long white counter with a group of phones on it, he grabs a blue school chair and sits down in front of a phone. About 30 seconds later, the phone in front of him starts ringing. Ashley yells to him," Pick it up."

Cadet Skyy sits there staring at the chessboard. Then he grabs a sheet of paper and a pencil.

Dear Reign

Just got your letter every time I get a letter, it makes being away from you a little easier. It's hard hearing that DJ is still messing with you and I can't be there for you, If I keep doing good I should have a Senior Cadet board in about a month, that is the last part of the program. It takes about a month to finish, if I do good then I can graduate and come home.

"Cadet Skyy, who do you want to call?"

"My mom." He continues writing, *I got a phone call so I will finish after I get off you know maybe you can be over the house when I call, and we can talk.*

JSO Ashley yells louder, "The phone is ringing."

Cadet Skyy gets up and slides the letter underneath the chessboard.

He shuffles to the ringing phone and grabs a seat. When he picks up the phone Vicky is already saying, "Hello, hello?"

"Mom it's me Jordan."

"Jordan it is so good to hear from you. How you doing?"

"I'm good just counting down the days till I go to the Sr. Cadet Board."

"So how many days do you have?"

"About 33, have you talked with Reign?"

"Well, she just dropped the letter off but we didn't talk. Why?"

"She wrote and her ex is still bothering her."

"She has not said anything to me about it."

KJ walks into the kitchen where Vicky is sitting at the table,

KJ excitedly, "Is that Jordan?"

Vicky nods her head yes, "KJ wants to talk to you." She hands the phone to him.

Cadet Skyy, "What's good KJ it's good hearing your voice, I can't remember the last time we talked."

"I don't know either, so what's it like there?"

In a more serious tone, "I hate it, we wear the same thing every day, we have to get our haircut bald every week, and they always yelling at us. Some of these fools in here are straight crazy. It's the same thing every day, I feel like I'm stuck in a movie. I got some stories I could tell you. You need to listen to mom you don't want to be locked up."

"So, when are you coming home?"

"Hopefully in two months, if I keep doing good." He takes a deep breath and continues, "I want to apologize to you about how I was acting--disrespecting mom, smoking in front of you, running the streets with Nick and Spenser not hanging with my lil bro."

KJ is confused about where all this is coming from, "Okay thanks."

"I just wanted to tell you while I had the chance. Hopefully, when mom comes to visit you can come too. Can you give the phone back to Mom?"

KJ hands the phone back to Vicky, "He wants to talk to you."

Vicky on the phone, "Everything okay?"

Cadet Skyy says, "Yeah we good I just needed to tell him something. So, you said you haven't seen Reign?"

"No, I can tell you're worried don't let this cause you any problems. You're doing good you can't do anything about whatever's going on with her. Don't worry about the things you can't control."

"So, you coming to see me this week?"

Vicky replies, "I won't be able to this week I have to take Ericka to see her father."

Cadet Skyy in a low tone, "I understand."

Vicky in her cheerful mom's voice encourages him, "It's not that bad, I'll definitely be there the next weekend. You can still call me."

"Okay, I got to go, bye." He hangs up.

CHAPTER FORTY-SIX

Recruit Workman is in Mrs. High's English class reading, "Romeo and Juliet." Recruit's Barnes and Gomez are sitting in front of him, all of them are in the back of the class. Mrs. High is sitting at her desk head buried in the book following along with the rest of the class as they read the play. Barnes is directly in front of him and Gomez to the left neither of them is paying attention to the play. Barnes pulls out his white school binder, flips it open, and in the front pocket is a picture of Cadet Skyy's girlfriend Reign. Workman is shocked to see this, he doesn't know whether to say something or see how it plays out. Barnes pulls the picture out, hands it to Gomez

"Check it out this is my girl." He whispers.

Gomez takes the picture, leans towards Barnes, "What's her name?"

"Reign."

Workman from behind taps, Gomez's left shoulder, "Yo can I see it."

Gomez hands him the picture, he just wanted to confirm what he already knew. It is Cadet Skyy's girl. He wonders, *how did he get it? Does Skyy know?*

JSO Erickson pokes her head in the class and yells, "Alright everybody fall out and get in formation."

Mrs. High stands up, "Class that's it for today remember where we stopped."

All the residents start to stand up and gather their schoolbooks, Barnes looks back at Workman and says, "Give me the picture."

He initially is hesitant about giving it back. He thinks about keeping it and giving it back to Jordan, but he didn't want any trouble with JSO Erickson there, so he gives the picture back and Barnes quickly puts it in his binder. He shuffles to get in formation, JSO Bentley calls out to the company, "Half step…" they respond, "Left foot…March" and they march out the building.

They enter the barracks marching in the square loudly calling cadence. Sgt. Crawford signals him to stop the company, Bentley calls out, "Company Halt!"

They respond, "Step place!"

Bentley yells out, "When I give the command to fall out, fall out to your squad bay and change over for PT… Fallout."

All the residents scurry into one of the four different squad bays, bumping into each other. Cadet Skyy and Recruit Barnes fall into Charlie squad bay and Recruit Workman goes into Bravo squad bay.

As he is changing into his blue PT shorts, he wonders how he is going to tell Cadet Skyy.

JSO Gilmore walks to the front of the barracks and begins the countdown 10…….9………8….

The residents start moving faster getting dressed and start coming out of their squad bays.

Sgt. Crawford, JSO's Towers, and Bentley walk up to the front beside Gilmore.

Recruit Workman waits for Cadet Skyy to fall into formation, he shuffles beside him in formation whispers to him, "I need to tell you something."

Cadet Skyy looks at him whispers back, "What's up?"

Gilmore yells,"1."

"Freeze Cadet Free" they all yell in unison.

The phone rings, JSO Gilmore shuffles back to get it.

Sgt. Crawford in front of the company yells, "All right we are about to do PT we are going to divide you up and a JSO will be leading each group.

JSO Gilmore yells from the back, "Cadet Skyy Mrs. Roebuck wants to see you in her office."

Recruit Workman looks at him, "I will get with you later come find me."

Cadet Skyy is curious about what is so urgent, turns asks, "What's up?"

Gilmore yells, "Go she is waiting on you."

He turns and shuffles out the door.

In Mrs. Roebuck's office, Cadet, Skyy sits in front of her while she is at her desk.

She stops typing on the computer looks at him says, "I called you up here to tell you some good news.

You are getting an extra 300 points enough so you can go to the senior cadet board two weeks earlier."

Cadet Skyy shocked by what he just heard, screams out an exuberant, "YES!" Then he asks, "Are you joking?"

Mrs. Roebuck replies, "No, you should know by now that I don't joke."

Cadet Skyy still excited asks the natural question, "Why am I getting these points?"

"Well, there are a couple of factors that come into play. One is timing we have a waiting list of prospective candidates to get into the program, so the director had us case managers come up with residents we think deserve a little extra help. Sometimes it's better to be lucky than good. You've been here seven months, the first couple of months you got off to a rough start, but you've come around. Now I don't know if you've truly made a change or if as the residents say you've 'fake it to make.' Only time and you can answer that. But I've talked with the JSO's, school teachers, case managers, even some of the residents, and everybody agrees that it appears like you made a change.

"So, will I be going, to a promotion board next week?"

"That is correct, any questions?" Cadet Skyy sits there quietly trying to take in what he just heard. "Ma'am no ma'am."

"Well if that's it. I'm calling the barracks to let them know you're headed back down."

Cadet Skyy steps outside and sees all the various groups doing PT with their JSO's. He is looking for Recruit Workman he is going to join up with that group to see what he needs to talk about. He spots him on the other side of the field with JSO Towers. He thinks, *Ain't nothing he can do to mess me up after that news.* He takes off across the field.

CHAPTER FORTY-SEVEN

"Cadet Skyy reporting as ordered sir."

JSO Towers looks over at him and says, "Fall in you got a lot of catching up to do."

He shuffles over right beside Recruit Workman and starts stretching as he is in the middle of doing some push-ups. He asks Workman, "Yo what do you need to tell me?"

Recruit Workman is trying to catch his breath as he is doing push-ups," We can talk after PT."

Towers tell Cadet Skyy, "We are doing pyramids. The first two exercises are lunges and mountain climbers, after that you will do crunches and leg lifts, the final exercise is push-ups and raise the roof to work your arms." He then turns his attention to the new recruits. "For the uninformed, a PT pyramid is you do fifteen lunges, then fifteen mountain climbers, back to fourteen lunges down to one for all the exercises."

Towers looks around at all the residents in his group, sees everybody is putting forth good effort claps his hands, "Good job, good job... keep it up."

He looks at Cadet Skyy, "Alright let's get cracking."

Cadet Skyy starts doing the lunges making a concerted effort to do the exercise correctly, he has noticed a change in his body since he has been at boot camp, he is not necessarily bigger but he has gained some muscle definition and his cardio has improved he remembers back to his first time running and not being able to make a complete lap around the track without walking. Now he is knocking out the first groups of exercises, without breaking a sweat, the other residents in the group are now finishing up. Some of them are stretching others are just sitting around horse playing with each other.

After another 20 minutes Sgt. Crawford blows the whistle yells, "POA move," everybody jumps to attention. "Alright PT is over; my group and Bentley's will go to the chow hall and eat. Towers and Gilmore's groups will go to the barracks for free time. "

Towers to his group, "Everybody fall in," they all fall in their columns of two. Cadet Skyy makes sure to fall in right beside Recruit Workman.

Workman already knows what he is about to asks says, "I'll let you know what's up once we start free time."

Cadet Skyy doesn't say anything, just nods in agreement.

Gilmore marches his group over to Towers, in his group is Recruits Barnes and Gomez. The groups join up together and march into the barracks.

JSO Gilmore addresses the two squads, "We about to do free time, and I will be doing head calls and Towers will be doing phone calls. Fallout."

There is a mad scramble, some of the residents go into the squad bay others go to the bathroom line.

Cadet Skyy goes to the table and sits down, he is not tired since he only did 20 minutes of PT.

Recruit's Gomez and Barnes go to the bathroom line, Recruit Workman goes to his squad bay to get his library book. He shuffles over to the table and sits down in front of Cadet Skyy.

Cadet Skyy looks at him, "So what's up bro? What did you have to tell me that was so important?"

Recruit Workman looks back at him tells him, "When we were in school today in Mrs. High's class Barnes pulled out the picture of your girl Reign from his school binder."

Cadet Skyy is stunned by this asks, "Isn't he in the S.O. squad (sexual offender)? Are you sure?"

"Yeah, he is bro. He showed it to Gomez then he showed it to me and said it was his girl."

Cadet Skyy doesn't say anything, he suddenly blurts out, "Sir Cadet Skyy requests permission to go to the squad bay, sir."

Towers yells, "Sure go-ahead."

He gets up shuffles to his squad bay, looks underneath his rack in his storage bin, he pulls it out, and looks through the letter that the picture was sent with, but the picture is not there. He then goes through all his mail and cannot find the picture. He gets up and goes to Recruit Barnes's storage bin and he sees his school binder opens it up and in the front pocket is Reign's picture. He grabs the picture walks out of the squad bay, heads straight towards Barnes, and yells, "What the fuck you doing with my girlfriend's picture?"

Barnes who is sitting at the table playing cards with Gomez is stunned. Recruit Workman gets up and grabs, Skyy from behind by his left arm to hold him back, and cautions, "Chill bro."

JSO Gilmore is finishing monitoring the bathroom breaks, rushes over gets in between Barnes, and Skyy yells, "What's going on?"

Cadet Skyy looks at JSO Gilmore points at Barnes, holds up the picture, "He took this picture of my girlfriend from my free time stuff."

JSO Gilmore looks at Barnes asks, "Is this true?"

Barnes, attempting to look as innocent as possible says quietly, "Sir no sir."

Skyy hearing him lying gets louder, "He's lying sir you can ask Recruit Workman."

JSO Towers walks over to the commotion, "What's going on?"

JSO Gilmore asks Recruit Workman still standing there, "So what do you know about this?"

Recruit Workman answers, "In Mrs. High's class Barnes pulled out that picture and showed it to me and Gomez. I know it's Skyy's because he showed it to me and Cadet Waddles when he got it in the mail."

Everybody looks at Barnes, Towers asks, "Is this true?"

Barnes feeling the pressure puts his head down answers, "Yeah he showed it to me in class."

Gilmore asks, "So Barnes I'm going to ask you again. Is this your picture?"

Barnes drops his head down and answers, "Sir no sir."

JSO Towers tells Barnes, "Ok get up you're going to the brig for having the property of another resident without permission. He looks at Gilmore, instructs him, "Take him to the brig." They both walk away.

JSO Towers looks at Cadet Skyy, "So what were you going to do to Barnes?"

Cadet Skyy surprised by the question, "Um sir I don't know just wanted to find out why he had my girlfriend's picture."

"You were coming at him aggressively, maybe you need to go to the brig for a relations with other situation, instigating a fight, I'm putting you in the brig."

CHAPTER FORTY-EIGHT

Cadet Skyy in a panicky voice, "Sir I didn't do nothing I was just asking him why he has my girlfriend's picture. I got a Sr. Cadet Board next week; I can't go the brig."

"Come on let's go you should have thought about that before you did this." JSO Towers replies, showing not an ounce of empathy.

Cadet Skyy can feel anger boiling up inside, but he knows he must control it, getting emotional would completely destroy any chance he has of avoiding the brig. As they are slowly walking towards the brig, he does something he hasn't done too many times he pleads, "Please sir, I'll do any emi you want me to I just can't go the brig." As they walk to the brig, JSO Gilmore is filling out the paperwork for Barnes. Cadet Skyy with tears forming in his eyes stops and pleads with Gilmore, "Sir can you talk to him, Mrs. Roebuck told me that I am getting some extra points so I can go to the board, if I go to the brig, I won't go." Gilmore stares at him and sees the desperation in his face, points to a spot by the laundry room, "Go over and start doing some eight-count bodybuilders."

Skyy shuffles to the spot and start's doing the emi.

Gilmore looks at Towers asks, "Do we need to place him in the brig?"

Towers replies, "He went after Barnes like he was going to hit him we don't know what would have happened if Workman hadn't stopped him."

Gilmore continues to fill out the paperwork, "Your right but he didn't hit him, and you got to admit that Skyy has changed a lot from when he first got here."

Towers reluctantly agreeing, "I've noticed it, but it still doesn't change what he did today."

"Point, but when he first got here if you told him he was going to the brig, he would cuss you out, get all up in your face, and have to be restrained. Look how he handled it today, we see he is trying we need to show him that we will work with him if he gives us a reason to."

Towers looks over at Cadet Skyy doing the exercise, sweat forming on his forehead and shirt he's breathing hard as he pauses for a few seconds and starts back at it again.

Towers demands, "Get over here Skyy."

Cadet Skyy shuffles over to him stand at the position of attention breathing heavily catches his breath, "Sir yes Sir."

"Look I know we haven't always seen eye to eye but in the end, it's not personal. I don't mind testing some of y'all to see how you are going to respond that's my job. With that being said, I'm not going to place you in the brig. You can thank Mr. Gilmore for that, after talking with him he pointed out to me that you've changed and that if you made the effort we need to do the same thing. Just so you know you will be doing e.m.i from now until we go to the rack.

You think you're sweating now I want sweat dripping off you like you just ran a marathon before you're finished."

Cadet Skyy smiling excitedly yells, "Sir thank you. Anything you want me to do right now?"

Cadet Towers with a smirk on his face, "You keep smiling I might just put you in the brig anyway, go away and start doing some mountain climbers and push-ups."

CHAPTER FORTY-NINE

Vicky and Ericka are sitting on the floor putting the finishing touches on the puzzle when Vicky's phone alarm starts buzzing. She looks at it and it's four p.m. She stands up stretches her arms overhead, and says, "It's time for us to go visit Jordan." She yells, "KJ get ready it's time to go see Jordan."

KJ comes out of his room and asks, "Do I have to go? Dre asked if I could come over to his house."

Vicky surprised asks, "So how come you don't want to go see him?"

KJ stands there looks at her, "I saw him 2 weeks ago," he takes a deep breath and sighs, "I don't like going there and I don't like seeing him locked up."

Vicky looks at him and takes a deep breath, "I understand I don't want to force you if you don't want to go." She looks at Ericka who is still sitting down working on the puzzle asks, "So do you want to go?"

Ericka looks up and eagerly replies, "Yes I want to see him, I haven't seen him since he's been gone."

Vicky looks back at KJ, "So what are you and Dre going to be up to?"

KJ responds, "We are going to play Madden."

Vicky looks at her phone, "Well ok I don't want to be late; I will drop you off at Dre's on our way. Let's go."

In the chow hall for lunch, the residents are lined up in four separate columns ten residents in each column, there are 8 different tables 15 feet long, each side fits seven residents. Cadet Waddles in formation at the front of the line turns his head looks over his left shoulder yells extra loudly, "One step forward... march."

He then takes one step off his left foot and goes to pick up his tray as the residents behind him all step off in unison with their left foot. If everybody does it together, it looks impressive. Today's meal is spaghetti with meatballs, two slices of white bread, green beans, apple dump cake for dessert, and their choice of chocolate or white milk and a glass of water. He gets his tray and walks to the table where all the residents are standing up still holding their trays. Cadet Waddles is the last resident, he assumes the same position as the residents at the table.

JSO Knight is a new 5'10" blond-haired white male JSO that's been there for one month. He is in his mid-20's and is standing at the head of the table. He's a former military veteran and has a cocky attitude, to go along with his high and tight haircut. He yells, "Trays... down!"

All the residents lean down and place their trays down together making one, "Clicking" sound.

Knight orders, "Sit down."

All the residents immediately sit down and begin to eat. There is no talking allowed at the table.

This process continues until all the residents are eating.

The cook asks, "How many residents are in the brig?"

Sgt. Dell answers, "Three."

"Okay, their trays should be ready in 15 minutes."

The phone rings Sgt. Dell gets up and answers the phone after a 20-second conversation, he hangs up and walks back to his tray, "Skyy you got a visit."

JSO Knight, who is sitting at the same table as Skyy asks, "I hear you got a Sr. Cadet board Monday?"

Skyy excitedly answers, "Sir yes sir."

Knight mumbles, "Man I guess they'll let anybody be a Sr. Cadet these days."

He hears the comment but doesn't respond, thinks *this dude has been here a month, and thinks he knows me, haters gonna hate.*

He starts shoveling the food in his mouth, he is excited to tell his mom about the Sr. Cadet board. When they talked three days ago he didn't mention it because he wanted to tell her in person to see her reaction.

After three minutes he is finished. He places his plastic spork in the cup and comes to the sitting position of attention. "Sir Cadet Skyy request permission to dump."

Knight without looking up replies, "Go ahead."

He dumps his tray, shuffles over to Sgt. Dell and says, "Sir Cadet Skyy request... Dell interrupts him, "Go ahead."

Cadet Skyy is in the visitation room, with Vicky and Ericka they are sitting beside each other. He is very excited, to see Ericka since this is his first time seeing her in months. She is smiling ear to ear, just so happy to see him.

She reaches over and feels his right arm, "Wow you're getting some muscles."

He flexes his arm in the classic muscle man pose to show off his biceps.

Vicky looks at him smiling, shaking her head approvingly, "You look good this place has helped you out a lot."

Jordan asks, "So where is KJ?"

Ericka blurts out, "He didn't want to come he went over to Dre's house."

Jordan has a disappointed look on his face, Vicky sees this, she explains, "There's more to it than that, Dre asked if he could come over and play Madden. He says he doesn't like seeing you like this."

Jordan just shrugs it off, asks Ericka, "So what you been up to girl?"

"Nothing, just school, and me hanging with Zoey."

Jordan with a puzzled look on his face asks, "Who?"

"Your girlfriend's sister."

Jordan smiles answers, "Oh ok we all went to play basketball together I remember now."

Jordan looks at his mom asks, "So have you heard anything from her?"

Vicky looks back at him, shakes her head no, "I've reached out to her after we talked on the phone, but she never answered back."

Ericka replies, "When I go over there and hang out with Zoey, she is mostly in her room sometimes she has some friends over."

Jordan looks at Ericka with an interested look, "Boy or girl?"

Ericka answers, "Just some other girls, I think they are her teammates."

Vicky assures him, "After we leave today, I will text her again to tell her we visited. So, what's been up with you?"

Jordan excitedly answers, "I almost forgot I'm going to the Senior Cadet Board next week."

Vicky equally excited jumps out of her chair, "Yes! Praise the Lord!" Jordan stands up and she gives him a big hug. Squeezing his neck, she replies, "Congratulations, that's great news." They both sit down.

Jordan tells her, "Mrs. Roebuck told me a few days ago they were giving me some extra points so I can go the board. "

Ericka excitedly asks, "So that means you get to come home?"

Jordan answers, "No it's the last thing I have to do before I get to come home, if I don't have any more problems, I should be home in a month."

"Not unless you get some more extra points," Vicky adds.

Jordan looks at her and grins, "OK not let's get carried away."

Vicky laughs, "You never know! You didn't know about these points, and yet you got them, it just goes to show that if you do good things, good things come back at you. Why did they give them to you?"

"Well, she said they have a waiting list of residents trying to get in and they have to make space, all the case managers, JSO's thought I was doing good and deserved the chance."

Vicky stares at Jordan as she smiles from ear to ear. She is just so happy, that he is doing so much better especially with all the trouble he had when he first got there.

She asks, "So when is the board?"

Jordan replies, "It's Monday morning. They ask all the staff and some of the residents if they think you should be a senior cadet. There is an oral test that you have to do."

Mr. Grayson from his office yells, "Visitation almost up you got five minutes."

Vicky complains, "I know that wasn't the full 30 minutes."

Mr. Grayson hears this gets up from his office walks over to their visitation, "I'm sorry you came so late, you're not going to get your full time."

Cadet Skyy looks at Mr. Grayson, "Sir I'm going to the Sr. Cadet Board next week."

Mr. Grayson tells him, "I heard, you deserve it. Well, say your goodbyes."

He walks away, all three of them stand up, Vicky says, "Well we got to be going to pick up KJ anyway. I'm so happy for you son. "

Cadet Skyy replies, "Thanks, mom." They hug.

He looks at Ericka, "Thanks for coming to see me, tell KJ I said what's up."

Ericka smiles at him. "I will."

He looks at Vicky, "Can you call Reign to let her know what's up?"

Vicky promises, "I will soon as we leave here, Love you."

Mr. Grayson standing outside his office watching, says to Jordan, "I'll let them know you are on your way down."

Jordan takes off, Mr. Grayson walks over and lets Vicky and Ericka out.

On the drive home, Vicky pushes the phone button on her steering wheel, finds Reign's number, calls, it rings four times, Reign answers, out of breath, "Hello."

Vicky responds," Hello, Reign is everything ok?"

Reign replies, "Oh yeah I'm good I'm just on my way to work."

Vicky says. " I just called; I haven't heard from you in a while."

Reign sighs, "I'm sorry, between basketball playoffs, and my job I've just been doing a lot."

"So how is basketball?"

"It's over we lost in the second round of the playoffs. Now I got a new job at the Hoops and Hops shoe store. What's up?"

Vicky excitedly replies, "I got some good news, I just came from visiting Jordan today, he's going to Sr. Cadet Board, next week."

"So that means he gets to come home?"

Ericka listening butts in, "I asked the same thing."

Reign says, "Oh what's up Ericka? I didn't know you were there."

Vicky responds, "No it's just the last phase before he gets to come home. He said it should take a month."

Reign excited, "That's great, I miss him so much."

Vicky replies, "Yeah I do too, I'm praying nothing else happens to mess him up. So, is everything ok *with you? Jordan mentioned something about your ex messing with you?"*

Reign pulls into the Hoops and Hops parking lot she is not comfortable talking about it, *"Everything is good he approached me after a game we talked a little no big deal."*

"Okay, I was just asking Jordan was worried."

Reign *gets out of her car, "I haven't seen or heard from him since that night, so everything is good. I got to go I'm at work."*

"Ok, I will keep you posted. She hangs up.

Vicky tells Ericka, "It was good hearing from her, Okay let's text KJ to let him know we are on the way."

Dre and KJ are on Dre's living room couch playing NBA 2K on Dre's PS4, Dre gets a text from Cage, *you want to come by and shoot some hoops?*

Dre looks at the text asks KJ, "Yo Cage just texted me he wants to ball at his house, you down?"

KJ pauses the game, "Yeah I'm getting bored, I've been playing all day."

Dre gets up off the living room couch, "Cool." He texts: *KJ is with me otw.*

At Cage's house, he has a two-car wide driveway with one of those outdoor adjustable basketball goals sitting in between the two garage doors.

Cage is already outside shooting on the goal. Cage sees them walking up, "What's up bros?"

They walk up and Cage passes the ball to Dre, "Let's run a 21."

Dre catches it dribbles to the edge of the street, yells, "Ball up."

It's starting to get dark so, they stop, playing, they all just sit in the driveway in front of the basketball goal.

Cage gets up opens the garage door there are no cars parked in it at the time, the inside is set up like a woodshop, with 2 lawn mowers on the left side and a gray metal shelf, holding various sizes of clay planters.

Cage walks to the shelf squats down and underneath the bottom, shelf pulls out a bag with weed and a black and white striped 'spoon' smoking pipe.

He walks back to Dre and KJ and takes a seat. He packs the pipe, asks Dre, "You want to hit this?" As he lights it up.

Dre surprised answers, "I didn't know you smoked?"

Cage taking a hit answers, "Everybody smokes."

Dre answers, "Nah I'm good."

KJ spontaneously answers, "I'll hit it."

Dre is surprised as Cage passes him the pipe. KJ takes the pipe, inhales, and immediately coughs intensely, Cage laughs says, "First time huh?"

KJ nods his head in agreement he gives the pipe back to Cage who packs more weed in it.

KJ still recovering from the hit says, "No more I'm good. I just wanted to get a hit."

Cage asks, "So what does it feel like?"

KJ looks at him, "Nothing really."

Dre looks at his phone and stands up, "I'm about to be out of here you coming KJ?"

KJ stands up and replies, "Yeah we need to be getting back to your place."

Cage still sitting down, takes another hit of the pipe. "All right bros I'll get with you later."

On the way, back KJ gets a text from his mom: *just to let you know we're home.*

CHAPTER FIFTY

Monday morning 0900 hrs. Cadet Skyy is standing outside the conference room, at the position of attention and he is nervous, his heartbeat elevated the anticipation is killing him. He thinks, *be confident, you got this, keep cool and everything will work out.*

A male's voice booms out, "Cadet Skyy step in here."

He walks in and immediately comes back to the position of attention, confidently sounds off with, "Cadet Skyy reporting to the board as ordered."

In front of him is a long eight-foot table, with the case managers sitting behind it in this order, Mrs. Kirkland on the left, Mr. Grayson at the center, and Mrs. Roebuck on the right.

Mrs. Roebuck is the first to talk, "Good morning Cadet Skyy today is your Sr. Cadet board, you can be at ease."

He relaxes and spreads his feet shoulder-width apart and places his hands behind his back.

She continues, "To explain the process we passed out a board sheet to the JSO's and they voted yes or no whether they believe you should be a Sr. Cadet. We are also for the first time is giving some of the residents a chance to vote and see what your peers think of you. Now of course your peer's vote won't decide if you pass or not but we think it is a good way to access you're standing with your fellow residents. Mrs. Kirkland will discuss the JSO vote sheet now."

Mrs. Kirkman picks up a piece of paper off the desk, looks it over for a few seconds. She looks up at Cadet Skyy, "I will tell you we had twelve JSO's who voted, and out of the twelve nine gave you a yes and two a no and one who marked between the yes and no, I'll take that as an undecided. Now I'm not going to tell you how each JSO voted, I will just read a few comments to see what you think? Any questions?"

Cadet Skyy answers, "Ma'am no ma'am."

"Ok, let us begin, some of the yes comments include, *"Has made a real change."* Another comment was, *he made some good progress from when he first got here, Skyy is an example of why we have this program.* Somebody just *wrote hell, yes a few more just checked yes without any comment.*

Now for the no comments, *"Believes he is faking it to make it"* and the other comment," got a lot of extra points to push him through the program." The yes/no vote says, *"Not sure if he has changed or not."*

Mrs. Kirkland looks at him and asks, "Do have anything you want to say?"

Cadet Skyy thinks for a moment wanting to answer in the most mature way possible says, "No not really I just appreciate all the staff that voted yes, and for the ones who voted no everybody has a right to their opinion."

Mrs. Kirkland, "All right thank you straight to the point. Mr. Grayson, you're up."

Mr. Grayson comments, "Thank you, as Mrs. Roebuck explained earlier we are trying something new with your peers having a vote since there are fifty-four residents currently in the program we are not going to read all the comments just the overall votes. We realize that some of them might not vote objectively, so we just want an overall feel for what your peers think about you."

He looks over the sheets, "There are forty yes votes and eight no votes, six residents who we didn't let vote because they haven't been here long enough."

Mr. Grayson, "Any comments."

"I guess it's cool my most of my peers are down for me."

Mr. Grayson puts the paper down, "Well ok. Mrs. Roebuck has the final part."

Mrs. Roebuck looks directly at him, "Before we get to the last part we checked how you are doing in school and you are passing your classes and Mr. Grayson says you are on track to pass his anger management so everything is good there. This last section entails three verbal questions that I'm going to asks you. We are going to give you time to think about your answer, are you ready for the first question?"

Cadet Skyy, "Okay."

"Why do you deserve to be a Sr. Cadet?"

Cadet Skyy standing there rolls his eyes to the ceiling as he ponders his answer, after about one minute he answers. "Because I had a hard time when I first came here, I didn't think I could do it, but all the staff working with me help me realize that I could if I put my mind to it, and with the problems I had since I've been here I think I could be a good example for some of the other residents who are having a difficult time."

Mrs. Roebuck tilts her head up signaling, okay not bad, she asks the next question, "How has this program helped you?"

Cadet Skyy answers without thinking, "It's taught me that it is not always about me and what I wanted. That I was a selfish person only concerned about myself. That I need to think about other people especially my family."

Mrs. Roebuck's final question, "What from this program have you learned that you can apply once you go home?

Cadet Skyy also answers this question quickly, "As I said before, I need to be more concerned about other people's feelings. That sometimes people are going to do stuff to try to get you angry, and that you should not always go with your first reaction because you could end up doing something stupid or dangerous and end up hurting someone."

Mrs. Roebuck states, "All good answers, well we are going to have you step outside and we are going to discuss it."

"Ma'am yes ma'am," he steps outside the conference room.

Sgt. Crawford's outside monitoring a classroom asks, "Did you pass?"

He looks at him and shrugs his shoulder quietly and answers, "I don't know."

Sgt. Crawford replies, "Well good luck, and you got it."

Cadet Skyy stands there leaning against the wall for another four minutes.

Mr. Grayson loudly, "Cadet Skyy come back in here."

He stands back up takes a deep breath and steps back in.

Mrs. Roebuck stands up says with a joyous tone announces, "Congratulations you're a Sr. Cadet."

CHAPTER FIFTY-ONE

Sr. Cadet Skyy is sitting proudly in his gold Sr. Cadet shirt for his final anger management class with Mr. Grayson. The classroom is set up in a semi-circle with the teacher's desk in the front, Mr. Grayson is leaning on the desk, and the eight residents are sitting in blue school chairs facing him.

Mr. Grayson looks at Sr. Cadet Skyy, "I have a question I like to asks all the students before they complete this course, "How are you going to apply what you learned once you leave?"

Everybody turns and looks at Sr. Cadet Skyy who feels the pressure, he thinks for one minute finally says, "To keep it 100, I know I'm going to have to work on these steps, but if something pops off, the first thing I'm trying to do is take deep breaths to relax and count to ten. While I'm doing this, hopefully, this will give me the chance to bring down my energy. If that doesn't work and if possible, I will walk away from the situation."

Mr. Grayson shakes his head in agreement. Still leaning on the front of the desk he says, "You got to remember you getting angry here, there is an immediate consequence EMI, counseling, or even the brig. Out there the consequences may not be as fast, so you may get away with it longer until something bad happens. Also, even though you're attempting to change the people and situations you encounter will be the same. It is how you deal with the people or situations that's different to show if you have changed."

He turns around and picks up a piece of paper off the desk and says, "Sr. Cadet Skyy come up here."

Sr. Cadet Skyy gets up and walks to the front and stands to the left of Mr. Grayson.

Mr. Grayson reads from the paper, "This is a Certificate of Completion of the Allen County Juvenile Anger Management for Jordan Skyy signed by me and Mrs. Roebuck.

He hands the certificate to Sr. Cadet Skyy, he smiles, and the residents give him a lackluster golf clap.

Tristan and Dejuan are hanging out at the Town Center. They are walking to Tristan's car; they pass by the Hoops and Hops sports store Dejuan looks through the window and sees Reign assisting a female customer and a little boy. Dejuan walks towards the store.

Tristan asks, "Yo fool where you going?"

Dejuan responds, "I'm just going to say what's up."

"Didn't you tell me she said she was going to call the cops next time she sees you?"

Dejuan walks to the door. "Bro that was about a month or two ago that's old. Are you coming?"

Tristan shuffles towards him. "Why not? I love seeing Reign shade you."

They walk into the store, there are small displays of various men's and women's athletic shoes, in the front part of the store, as they walk past these Reign is still busy with her customers and does not notice them. They walk down the men shoe's aisle. Tristan is looking at different basketball shoes while DJ is just fiddling around keeping an eye on Reign.

"Is there anything I could assist you with?" A young red-headed salesman asks.

Dejuan turns looks at him, "Naw dog we good."

He gives them a smarmy smirk, turns around, "Ok just let me know if you need any help," he replies as he walks away.

By this time Reign and her customers are walking towards the register, DJ continues to watch her while Tristan is trying on shoes, he has no plans on buying.

As soon as the lady and her son pay for her shoes and walk to the door. DJ quickly walks up to the register.

Reign looks up from the register, she is not too surprised, "What are you doing here? I thought you finally realized the truth."

"Me and Tristan were hanging out and we walked by and saw you," he pauses, "Look I just want to say I'm sorry for what happened that night at the game."

Reign surprised," Okay I accept your apologies."

Tristan starts walking towards them, DJ asks, "Can we get together and talk sometime?"

Reign walks from behind the cash register, angrily answers, "I knew you were up to something with your fake ass apology."

DJ irritated by her reaction, "Why you coming off like that, I just want to talk with you, not at work…

She cuts him off, "That's right I'm at work so if you're not buying anything leave before I get into trouble and get fired."

Tristan walks up to DJ tells him, "Let's go, bro."

Dejuan and Tristan walk to the door, he stops and says, "I know where you work you'll see me around."

The young salesman who was watching the whole thing walks up to Reign and asks, "Who was that?"

Reign quiet for a moment finally comes out and says, "My stalker ex-boyfriend."

CHAPTER FIFTY-TWO

Graduation Day it's finally here! Sr. Cadet Skyy is lying in his rack looking at the ceiling, listening as the rain hits the roof.

He didn't sleep too well just so anxious about finally leaving boot camp. He hears the 1st shift JSO's coming in so he knows the day is about to begin.

JSO Erickson opens the squad bay door as the lights are coming on.

He jumps out of the rack. JSO Erickson is at the door smiles, and says, "I see someone is excited."

He shuffles past her to get in the headcount formation. After morning headcount, he goes to the bathroom for his personal hygiene. He then goes back to the squad bay to get dressed and square away his rack.

JSO Erickson still at the squad bay door, asks, "Have you finished your graduation speech?"

He answers," Yeah just going to go over it again to double-check."

She inquires, "Can I see it?"

He opens his binder and hands, JSO Erickson, his speech.

JSO Towers starts the countdown yells, "10.....9.... 8 all the residents start a mad scramble, as they tighten up their racks, get their school books, rush to get out before he reaches one.

4…3….2…1

"Freeze Cadet, Freeze," all 50 of them yell as they stand at the Position of Attention.

Sgt. Crawford loudly addresses the company, "We have a graduation today so we are going to do 30 minutes of free time. Then go to breakfast after that go straight to the gym for graduation then school."

JSO Erickson walks over to Skyy to give him his speech back she tells him, "This is a good speech."

He smiles and answers, "Ma'am thank you, ma'am," as she walks away.

"Company POA move!" Sgt. Crawford yells. They are formed up after breakfast getting ready to go to graduation.

He continues, "Everybody straighten your uniform up and check out your buddy to make sure they are squared away."

Sr. Cadet's Skyy and Waddles are in the front of the formation.

Waddles looks at him and ask, "You ready bro?"

Skyy takes a deep breath and answers back, "Let's do it. I never thought we would be leaving here at the same time."

"Me neither especially when I got here and you were in the brig."

"Thanks for helping me figure it out."

"No problem bro."

"All right, POA move." Sgt. Crawford yells.

"Half Step.... Left foot.... March." The company marches out of the chow hall.

"Here we go again... Sgt. Crawford's calling the cadence as the company marches into the gym with Sr. Cadets Skyy and Waddles leading the formation.

As they are marching in Sr. Cadet Skyy's sounds off. He sees Vicky with KJ and Ericka sitting on the front row. Ericka smiles at him and waves as the company is mark time marching. Sgt. Crawford calls out, "Company Halt!" They respond with "Step Place and stop marching.

Sgt. Crawford steps to the front of the formation to speak to the audience. There are about 25 people in the audience mostly staff and teachers. Sr. Cadet's Skyy family is on the right side of the front row and Sr. Cadet Waddles' family is on the left side of the front row.

Sgt. Crawford says, "Good morning, I would like to thank you all for coming out on such a dreary day. Welcome, to the Allen County Boot camp for the graduation of Senior Cadet Waddles and Skyy. Well, let's get it started. Who is presenting Sr. Cadet Skyy for graduation?"

JSO Towers walks to the front of the audience. "Good morning ladies and gentlemen, I have the honor to present Sr. Cadet Skyy for graduation today. I will be the first to admit, I was shocked when Skyy asked if I would give him away especially when you consider our history. I was unsure at first but I thought if he is mature enough to put our history behind him, I should be able to do the same. After our first meeting when Sr. Cadet Skyy ended up having to be restrained, I never imagined he would graduate from this program, but he slowly started to figure it out and here we are today, he is a testament to why this program exists. I present Sr. Cadet Skyy. He turns and walks to Skyy shakes his hand and then goes back to the rear of the formation.

Sr. Cadet Skyy steps out of formation and goes to the center of the audience and pulls a piece of paper out of his pocket looks down at the paper and starts reading.

"Good morning ladies and gentlemen. I would like to thank you for coming to my graduation. I'm not sure where to begin." He looks up and sees his mother smiling from ear to ear which causes him to break into a smile. He looks back down and continues, "When I first got here I did not want to do this program. To be honest, I didn't think it was fair I was even here. I went to the brig my second day here. I was there for about a week, I didn't care I wasn't going to do the program. After I got out I started hanging with some residents like me who didn't care. We even talked about trying to escape, and I went to the brig again this time for almost two weeks. While in the brig I had a lot of time to think and I remember something my momma told me before I got locked up. 'The definition of insanity is to keep doing the same thing over and expecting a different result.' This is exactly what I was doing I guess I was crazy. When I finally got out I slowly started making some points. My case manager Mrs. Roebuck gave me some extra points to encourage me, and it showed me that if you do good, people are willing to help. The big thing that kept me going was my family. No matter how much trouble I was having or how stupid I was acting my mother never gave up on me." He looks up at her and she has tears in her eyes. He looks back down and continues, "As I started doing the program it became easier. I would like to thank the following staff JSO's Bentley, Ashley, Erickson, Gilmore, Towers, and even the haters... Mr. Knight. The two Sgt's Crawford and Dell. Case managers Mr. Grayson and Mrs. Kirkland and my Case Manager Mrs. Roebuck. The school teachers Mrs. High, Mrs. Trotman, Mrs. Underwood, and Mr. Booker. Last but not least I especially want to thank my mom for not giving up on me even though I gave her plenty of reasons to. And even though she is not here I want to thank my girlfriend Reign for holding it down, she kept me motivated. Finally, my experiences here at boot camp have greatly affected my life. As I stand before you today I promise you this will be the last time I will be locked up and I promise this will be the last time I will cause my family shame and sorrow because of my behavior." He looks up from the paper and folds it puts it in his pocket. He says, "Thank you." He walks back to the formation. Vicky stands up with tears in her eyes and claps, the rest of the audience claps loudly behind her.

The company marches out of the gym after graduation. Sgt. Crawford and JSO Erickson immediately come back in. Jordan and Joey are talking saying their goodbyes. As they approach Sgt. Crawford says, "Just wanted to say goodbye and good luck to the both of you. Stop by and see us some time to let us know how you're doing."

Joey replies, "Well sir I live about two hours away and I hope to never see you again.'

JSO Erickson laughs, Sgt. Crawford jokingly yells, "Push" to Waddles he immediately gets down and starts doing push-ups. After about five push-ups, Sgt. Crawford says, "Recover." He jumps to his feet and they shake hands.

Jordan looks at Erickson and tells her, "Thank you for everything you did for me."

Erickson replies, "I'm just glad you made it, you have too much going on to waste your life being locked up."

Sgt. Crawford tells both of them, "Well we have to get back to the company." He and Erickson leave, Jordan calls out, "Can you send in Mr. Towers?"

Sgt. Crawford answers, "Will do."

Mrs. Roebuck walks up to Jordan very emotionally she says, "I couldn't let you leave without saying goodbye."

Jordan looks at her and says, "I wouldn't've been able to do this without your help. Thank you."

Mrs. Roebuck overcome with emotion suddenly hugs him says, "You be good and let us know how you're doing."

Vicky tells Mrs. Roebuck, "I also would like to personally thank you for everything you did for Jordan."

Mrs. Roebuck replies, "He made me earn my paycheck, but in the end, it was worth it for days like this."

JSO Towers walks in.

Mrs. Roebuck, "Alright you take care, and hopefully, you meant what you said in your speech."

Jordan smiles and answers, "Ma'am yes ma'am."

JSO Towers approaches says, "Sgt. Crawford told me you wanted to speak to me?"

Jordan still in boot camp mode, "Sir yes sir. I just wanted to thank you for not putting me in the brig over my girlfriend's picture."

In a serious tone, he answers "Don't thank me I would have gladly put in had gotten stupid with me."

JSO Towers extends out his hand, Jordan extends his hand and they have a firm handshake.

"Take care Skyy." He walks away.

Vicky is driving home in light rain right after graduation with KJ and Ericka in the back. Vicky tells Jordan, "It is so good to have you home."

"I'm done with that place. I don't want to talk about boot camp."

Vicky asks, "What do you think about us having a little get-together? To celebrate you graduating boot camp."

"That's cool. I just want to see Reign."

"I know she has to work today."

Jordan inquires," Do you know what time she gets off?"

"No, but she normally gets off around nine."

He turns around and looks at KJ asks, "So what's been up, little bro?"

KJ answers, "Nothing. Going to school playing ball."

"So, you think you can beat me?"

"Probably I've gotten a lot better since you been locked up."

Jordan laughs says, "Just because I've been locked up doesn't mean I ain't been playing."

Vicky asks again, "So you sure you want to have a small party?"

Jordan thinks about it, nods his head. "It will be cool to see my bros."

Vicky smiles says, "Alright I'll drop you and KJ at the house. Ericka and I are going to run to the store to get some snacks."

Jordan looks back at KJ asks, "Can I get your phone I want to text Spencer and Nick that I'm home."

It's 8:30 p.m. Jordan and KJ are at home playing the PlayStation game "Call of Duty."

KJ's phone buzzes, he picks it up looks at it. It's a text from Nick, he hands the phone to Jordan and pauses the game.

Nick's text: *What up? Good to have you back, what time do you want me and Spens to come through?*

Jordan: *Anytime is good my mom's at the store picking up some snacks, I'm here with KJ just playing the station.*

He puts the phone down and asks KJ, "Bro how am I getting more kills than you? I've been locked up for almost a year and still the champion."

"Shut up you ain't better than me I'm just having a bad game." He throws the controller on the floor.

Jordan laughs at KJ and picks up the controller, "Chill bro I'm just messing with you." He gives the controller back to him.

The phone buzzes and Jordan picks it up, it's a text from Reign.

Reign: *Hey babe glad you are home can't wait to see you. I'm on my way home from work, should be there in 15 minutes.*

Jordan texts back: *I can't wait to see you Luv you.*

He puts the phone down excitedly yells, "Yeah, Reign's on her way home." He picks up the controller, "I'm done after this round gotta go see Reign."

KJ replies, "I thought she was coming to the party."

Jordan answers, "She is I just want to spend some time with her alone before the party."

KJ laughs and teases, "Jordan's in loooove."

He laughs, "Whatever bro."

He puts the controller down and stands up, "Tell mom I'm at Reign's house, I'll be back in a few minutes. Oh, and if Nick texts back let him know it's cool to come through."

There is a light drizzle as Jordan walks down the street to Reign's house. He is both anxious and excited about seeing her again after almost a year.

As he walks towards the house he realizes he has never been to her house or even met her parents.

As he gets closer to her house he sees a boy walking down the driveway it's Dejuan.

Dejuan sees him walking up the driveway says arrogantly, "So you back home huh?"

Jordan walks up the driveway responds, "Yeah I just got home today."

DJ walks directly towards Jordan and stands in his way, "So what are you doing here? You remember the last time, don't you?"

Jordan's heart is beating like a drum as shakes his head yes. He is not so much scared as just nervous, he does not want any problems on his first night back. He responds with a serious tone, "Yeah, I remember you the reason I got locked up. I just came to see Reign. The question is what are you doing here?"

"Me and Reign had a thing before, you were locked up, and you know what's up." He lifts the right side of his shirt to show a pistol in his waistband.

Jordan nervously asks, "So you going to shoot me here?"

Dejuan confidently responds, "Why not just me and you and no witness." He reaches into his waistband and pulls out the gun.

Jordan remembering their last encounter pushes DJ to the ground the gun falls out of his hand about three feet away. Jordan takes off running down the driveway. Dejuan gets on his feet and picks up the gun and chases after Jordan.

Jordan's running down the street turns around and sees DJ is chasing after him.

DJ shoots wildly chasing after him.

Jordan hears the gunshots yells, "KJ! KJ!"

KJ's in the house still playing the game, barely hears his name.

He runs outside and sees Jordan running as he slips on the wet street he catches himself with his hands, and this allows Dejuan to catch up, just as Jordan regains his footing Dejuan comes up and shoots him twice in the back.

KJ runs up to Jordan lying face down in the wet street with two bullet holes in his back.

Dejuan still standing over Jordan points the gun at KJ. KJ looks at him with fear in his eyes. Dejuan pulls the trigger and it clicks, the magazine is empty. He looks at the gun then looks back at KJ he turns and runs away.

KJ looks down at Jordan as he is face down in the street, he is still alive, he turns him over, Jordan is gasping for air cries, "This is not right I get out of boot camp, and my first night I get shot."

KJ crying yells, "I'll get him! I swear I'll kill him!"

Jordan fading away whispers, "No promise me you're not going to do anything. I don't want to die."

KJ crying pleads, "I don't want you to die."

Jordan looks at KJ with tears in his eyes, "Don't make the same mistakes I did. Promise me."

His eyes close for The Last Time.

The story continues in **_You Never Said Goodbye._** Available on Amazon right now or get an autographed copy, for $20. Hit me at evwill64@yahoo.com with your info.

Acknowledgments

Two books published in less than a year. Who would have thought it? This is the idea that started it all. **The Last Time** was originally written as a small five-page play that I wanted to perform while I was a JSO in Juvenile corrections. I wrote **You Never Said Goodbye** first because after reading the ending of **The Last Time,** I began to wonder what happens to KJ after seeing Jordan getting killed in front of him and consequently how it affected the whole family. It was probably about halfway through **You Never Said Goodbye** that I realized that I needed to tell Jordan's full story in **The Last Time**. I would like to thank the following for making this book possible.

First and most importantly, I need to give praise and honor to our Lord and Savior **Jesus Christ.** It is through his mercy and grace I was able to complete this book. This was definitely more challenging than **You Never Said Goodbye.** I am so grateful and appreciative that he gave me the mental strength and patience to see this through.

Choctaw Casino and Resort or more precisely the third shift crew. I am truly grateful for the positive response and support I received from the different departments EVS, Drop Team, Money Room, Cashiers Cage, Beverage, and of course my department Security. Thanks for the support.

Karen Lowe my editor and proofreader. We used to work together at Grayson County a few years ago, we both decided to move on (perfect timing). She was always quick with the red pen when grading papers and I knew she would be the same with this. I appreciate you taking time out of your schedule to do this for me. Any mistakes that made it through are my fault.

Jason Raynor of **105 Publishing.** I reached out to you late in the process of this book and you and your company came through in a timely way with a great book cover. Thanks, I definitely will be utilizing your company in any future books I do.

A special shout out to Latonia Butler, even though she did not directly work on this title it was her guidance and help which enable me to do **You Never Said Goodbye** and without that, I would not be here today.

My wife **Gayla** for reading several different versions of this story and giving me feedback. I know sometimes it was a chore but the feedback was invaluable to complete the story.

You can reach me on **Facebook** with your thoughts and comments about this story.

Also, please leave a review on **Amazon**, preferably a 5-star review. All reviews are invaluable so they are greatly appreciated.

I never dreamed three books would come out of this story of KJ and his need for revenge over Jordan's death. In writing these books I have gotten attached to these characters and their journey and I felt like I would not be doing right by them if I did not complete their story, So I am excited to announce that I will complete the story in my next book aptly titled:

CLOSURE

Coming Early 2022.

Made in the USA
Monee, IL
04 January 2022

87932929R00187